BAN

Roger Claessens
Philippe Wiertz

Bank Branch Management

EDITIONS
promo*culture*

About the authors :

Roger Claessens
Lc. Sc. Comm & Fin.
Prof. U.B.I. Brussels (United Business Institutes)
Former Branch Manager CLBN Rotterdam
email: contact@rogerclaessens.be

Philippe Wiertz
Lc.Sc.Crim.
Regional Manager Citigroup, Belgium

*With our thanks to Mrs. Chrisitne Graham Vivian
for her valued assistance*

This book contains information obtained from authentic and highly regarded sources. Reprinted material is quoted and sources are indicated. Reasonable efforts have been made to publish reliable data and information, but the authors and the publisher decline responsibility for the validity of all materials or for the consequences of their use.

Legal library deposit n° 6432

This book is printed in Luxembourg on acid-free paper

Print Nr: 03 02 06

ISBN: 2-87974-069-X

Table of contents

Introduction

Being promoted to branch manager is often a bit like being thrown into deep cold water. We would not be too surprised if you received little by way of information on the expectations linked to the assignment and even if you did, probably little information on how to achieve them. Indeed expectations are tremendous, not just from the organisation which promoted you into that position, but also from your team and from your customers.

Based on our experience, we thought that writing this book would allow you to gain: …guess what? "Time" your most precious asset. We believe that if you master all aspects covered, you are already starting to work towards your next promotion!

The first thing you would probably do, after the traditional handshakes, is to look at the financial data, and especially so at the **anticipated revenues**! In all likelihood the second thing would be to wonder how you will be able to achieve all this. The answer is through **marketing.** But there is more to it than that. You have to plan first, i.e. determine your **goals**. Once you have done that you will need to **motivate** your staff to achieve those goals. On top of it all you will need to **control and audit** what you are doing. Last, but not least, you will have to **sell**, sell and sell again!

However, what about yourself? Did you think how you feel about it all? What you could do for yourself? **Why not start thinking about**

your own well-being first? Once that is done, you might move on to the well-being of your colleagues! What do you think? For that reason, we have selected six criteria, which are **key** to reaching this goal:

- Motivation
- Marketing
- Planning
- Revenues
- Control & Audit
- The sales process

The choice is not random. It is the result of experience, intuition and discussions on the issue: "Why is one branch different and better than another branch? " What makes the difference? Clearly, the conclusion is "people and systems". We have therefore selected three fields of activities directly related to people: motivation, marketing and the sales process. The other criteria are more related to organisational and systems aspects: revenues, goal setting and control.

The purpose of it all will be that you will reach your goals and manage to improve on a permanent basis the performance of your staff, yourself and your branch.

We selected **branch** management because despite the high levels of market penetration by the new technologies in the financial services industry, the branch remains the consumer preference. The branch continues to be the predominant channel and the most appropriate means through which to protect and develop customer relationships. E-banking has proven to be an additional channel in many instances and has not replaced the traditional, the so called "bricks and mortar" branch. However, the accent today is more on retailing than on retail banking, forcing branch managers to be more imaginative and entrepreneurial.

Most retail branches sell the same products, offer the same service, are organised more or less in the same way. Why would a potential customer go to one branch rather than another one? Is it pure coincidence? Why is one branch more profitable than another one? Is it a matter of customer base? Why would a person feel more "at home" in one branch rather than another? Is it due to the lay out? The straightforward answer will in all likelihood be a matter of customer focus. The customer comes first and the marketing mix (price, people, promotion, place, products) determines the variables of the relationship with the customer.

When retail branches sell intangible products the answer is still pretty straight forward. Those branches are selling service. Customers perceive service in, amongst others, the following terms: consistency, satisfaction, image, price, influence of the seller, influence of the sales staff and timing. However, amongst these items quite a few are the result of the way the branch is managed. Branch management is therefore essential in achieving the ultimate check on performance, i.e. a long lasting customer relationship.

Why focus on branch management? That is where it starts and where it ends, providing you bank on excellent products. We can reasonably assume that you have products, which qualitatively and competitively match the other products in the market. Your challenge therefore is to be seen as being different and better than the others. Meeting this challenge should be the goal of good, pro-active management.

Management is much more than getting organised. It is about establishing an environment, wherein people work together in an organised, effective and motivated way to optimise customer, employee and shareholder value.

Certainly, much more can be written about each chapter. However, we wish to provide a comprehensive and practical guide enabling you to start implementation immediately. We wish you good luck. Indeed, you need a lot of competence and a little bit of luck. Do not hesitate to write to us if you have any questions or if you wish to share your experience with us.

How to use this book? The text covers:

1st *Most subjects that a branch manager might have to consider*

2nd *Some management background which we have put in italic type and blocked.*

3rd *Some key points and tips which we have blocked.*

Motivation

Introduction

Motivation is and has always been a difficult and complex issue. It is a very personal issue. It is related to our basic needs as a result of our sense of belonging, consciousness and finally our need for self fulfilment. Most people use only a fraction of the talent and capabilities they could bring to their job, resulting in a lesser performance than they are capable of producing. Motivation is linked with encouraging your staff to make the fullest use of their time, their talents and their skills in order to achieve superior results.

> *You do not directly motivate people, they are motivated to fulfil the their basic human needs, which vary in degree or intensity from individual to individual. The manager's task is to create enabling and enhancing conditions where staff can see "what's in it" for them on condition they stretch themselves and close the gap between goals and performance.*

Motivation is vital because no matter how brilliantly you plan, you need people to implement and achieve the plan. A lot of your time will be taken up anyway by motivational issues. In order to gain time you might as well address it properly from the very start. Your success will depend on dedication and motivation.

In this part of the world, i.e. the European Union, motivating people is definitely a challenge in itself. Why? Because of the laudable but burdensome social security system! Roughly speaking, for one hundred units of salary most employees would pay a bit less than 50% of that in taxes and social security contributions (health care, pension plan and unemployment insurance). Consequently, their net pay would be slightly over 50 units. Needless to say, when they look at their pay slips they are not ecstatic. The employer is even less so, as he has to top up about 100 units for his participation in the system for the benefit of his employees. In conclusion, the cost to the branch is about 200: salary 100 and additional contributions 100. It is easy to understand why a branch manager will think twice before hiring a person, especially bearing in mind that, cost apart, it is difficult and expensive to fire a person if that person does not match expectations. Secondly, minimum salaries are relatively high. Thirdly, if you grant a salary increase as a reward of good performance, it will cost the branch a substantial amount of money, whereas the employee will hardly see a difference in his or her pay cheque.

Needless to say, this situation is even worse for senior staff, whose bonus would be taxed in the highest bracket. In most circumstances these people would receive even less than 50% of the bonus.

So, the first conclusion is that money is not going to motivate people at a certain salary level. Then what is? How can you motivate people, who are no longer that sensitive to extra money? You could propose a company car? That is possible for senior management or eventually your branch managers but would be far too expensive for your employees. A bigger office? A better working environment? Why not? It is also an issue of branding. But would that do the trick? You need more than that. Fortunately, many studies have shown that money is often not the key motivator.

Rather, the key motivating factors for an individual are : achievement, recognition, responsibility and promotion. Of course this does not mean that money, status, security are not important. All of these things are but their weighting will be different. In any event, motivation is essential as a positive environment is imperative to achieving your goals.

But before discussing your staff, what about you as a branch manager? Are you happy? Have you assessed your strengths and weaknesses? Do you know what needs to be addressed first? How do you feel deep inside yourself? What about thinking just about you for a while?

Self assessment

Frequent and accurate assessment of progress is essential to improving effectiveness. This requires facts. Test all facts to ensure that they are accurate. If you set high standards for yourself, be sure to keep to them. **Be demanding on yourself**. Admit failings; and rectify them in order of priority. Stay calm, do not delude yourself and if you are successful stay alert as there are people around you who would not be averse to seeing you slip backwards. Always, always ask what you could have done better and how you could do it better. Be ready to take action as soon as it is feasible. Observe, adapt, change if need be. **The only thing which matters is striving for excellent day after day.** Concentrate on a particular goal and therefore dismiss anything which detracts you from this goal, such as, for instance, in-house politics. Do not be afraid of changing the course of action if that proves more effective in reaching your goal of excellence.

Have you considered what the qualities of an admired manager are and how close your method of working is to such a model?

How do you rate yourself, say, in?
- Communications skills
- Result or cost orientation
- Team building orientation
- Commitment to the organisation
- Integrity
- Courage
- Technical know how

The list could be much longer. Ask your staff to make such a list about you and you will immediately know what they expect from you! Of course, you might also ask them what they think their own list should be.

> *Working towards excellence presents a lifelong challenge and opportunity*

"The demands of the competitive marketplace have put such a premium on personal productivity that if you are not productive, you are out. The result is a tremendous pressure to perform, coupled with a sense of overwhelming insecurity about the future[1]".

---

1) Hyrum Smith, "Natural laws of successful time and life management", Time Warner, 1994.

Improving your personal skills

Undoubtedly, you will be reading quite a lot: call memos, credit requests, auditors' reports, senior management reports, marketing studies, product development fact sheets, and so much more. Do you know that you can train yourself to read faster and on top of it remember things better? The same goes for your memory. You can practice improving the percentage of retained information. You can also work on your communication skills, on your selling skills and so many other skills that are required to reach excellence.

There are quite a few specialised courses on these subjects. They may seem unnecessary but **in the final analysis a variety of skills will contribute as much as your formal academic training.** Never stop learning. Never stop improving. Never stop wanting the impossible in order to reach the possible.

One example: reading dynamics

We mentioned that you have to read a lot. How are you reading now? Do you pronounce mentally the words you are looking at or do you take a picture of the words, which are just in front of you? The difference in method will gain you seconds. Do you look at one word after the other sequentially or do you picture a group of words at the same time? Again, the difference will gain you seconds. Now, do you use your finger to underline the words you are picturing as a guide for your eyes? If you do, you will gain a few more seconds providing you guide your eyes and allow yourself to go faster over a text. You can even go further and train yourself to picture various lines of text at the same time! Let us say that you manage to save thus half an hour per day? Added up; it means almost one morning in a week!

If you master this methodology, you can start working on the memory improvement method, allowing you to remember information better. This requires that you go three times over one text in order to improve on the storage of information which you quickly pictured during your fast reading. 80% of the information is lost 24 hours after reading it. You therefore need to read it again after that time span, or even sooner.

The late president, John Kennedy, of the USA, was a well known fan of reading dynamics. If you want to measure your speed against a benchmark, the average speed is about 250-300 words per minute.[2] Graphs usually provide more information than text and can be more easily remembered.

Time management

Of all the resources at our disposal, time is probably the most valuable one. It is a scarce resource. Using time efficiently and effectively will contribute largely to the way your and the branch's overall performance is seen.

Start checking at the end of the day, how well you have used your time and how you can improve on its use. Have you started your day by listing your tasks? Have you prioritised the tasks? Have you covered all the tasks you aimed to cover?

Most importantly, what tasks could you have delegated and to whom? Are you certain all the tasks were really necessary in order to reach your objective? Did you leave a lot of unfinished tasks at the end of the day, which is going to make the next day even more hectic? Did you take some time to think about what you are supposed to be doing as well as your employees?

Make sure staff are aware of their cost to the company and the need by the company to offset that cost with income. Teach your staff to think like entrepreneurs. This means, you put money on the table, in this instance, the gross salary, and what do you get as a return? **Time is a cost or an investment opportunity.**

It is not just a managerial issue. Time and its use should be part of the culture of the branch. For instance, long hours do not necessarily mean working hard. How many of those long hours were wasted? In fact long hours are seldom very productive.

According to a study the biggest time robbers are: interruptions, putting off tasks till the next day, shifting priorities, poor planning and waiting for answers.

2)   Essential Manager's Manual, Robert Heller and Tim Hindle, Dorling Kindersley Ltd. UK, 1998

But the origin of those time eaters is even more interesting:

- unclear job definitions
- unnecessary meetings
- too much work
- poor communication
- disorganisation
- low morale
- untrained staff
- lack of authority
- too much travel
- mistakes
- revised deadlines
- failure to delegate
- poor attitude

- personal absentmindedness
- failure to listen
- indecision
- socialising
- fatigue
- lack of self discipline
- leaving tasks unfinished
- outside activities
- cluttered workspace
- unclear personal goals
- perfectionism
- attempting too much

Twenty five points of attention are listed. Tick off the list and rate yourself on 100 by multiplying your result by four. Thereafter highlight your priorities and you can start to aim at optimising time spent straight away.

A little tip! We talk about time management at work. You might also wish to consider time management of your spare time. Get as much out of it as you can!

Make sure your staff are also involved in time management be it only because of their impact on your time. The ultimate goal is that all are very well organised so that the whole branch becomes an example for others.

Finally, by improving on your listening skills, you will improve on the way you use your time. Therefore, make sure you listened to what was said, not to what you thought was said. Make sure you understand the background of what was said as well as the rationale for the communication in the first place. Give feed back so that you check your level of comprehension. Take notes and do not be afraid to summarise it all. Doing this as a matter of management style will make sure you get the maximum out of the time you decided to spend on an issue.

Effective selling

The situation ↓	Being on the same wavelength Know your customer's profile
The problem ↓	Give the customer time to express his problem
The information ↓	Provide as much information as possible to the customer so that the parameters of his problem become clear
The conclusion	The conclusion will be obvious if one has taken the time to go through all the preceding phases.

The above table summarises this very effective selling technique, which works whatever the subject of the sale, be it a financial product, a travel arrangement or a promotion.

This technique prevents impulse and it enforces structure, and above all it forces you to listen and to analyse. The method needs to be learned. It is not natural to behave like that. It is a matter of practice.

If you proceed too quickly, omit a phase, or do not possess all the information, you will create doubts or irritations or leave questions unanswered, which will prevent you from concluding the transaction.

After analysing hundreds of sales dialogues, it appears that born salespeople develop into exceptional salespeople through this method. The others become quite successful salespeople.

Never forget that we are permanently, one way or another, in a selling mode. We all have personal objectives that we wish to reach. All of us usually commit a double error: we do not pay attention and we dash too quickly to our goal, which provokes a corresponding resistance on the part of the purchaser, thus causing us to lose out on a favourable conclusion.

An interesting study about the difference between good and excellent salespeople provides for the following list of differences, as established by interviewed customers:

♦ An effort to understand the customer needs
♦ Presents logical arguments
♦ Provides evidence of product effectiveness
♦ Provides effective responses to objections
♦ Explains product drawbacks
♦ Is to the point
♦ Maintains eye contact
♦ Shows enthusiasm
♦ Understands economic conditions
♦ Can be trusted with confidential information
♦ Is sensitive to the customer's situation
♦ Is able to recapitulate accurately

This provides you with areas for attention, straight away!

Customers perceive the high performer as a genuine advocate of their needs even while he or she is actively promoting his or her company's position. A classical type of salesperson, extrovert, socially attractive, intuitive is not the preferred type anymore. Customers seem to appreciate more knowledge and discipline with the aptitude to demonstrate added value by communicating purposefully.

A further strength, in addition to those stated above, is not permitting yourself to be tempted to skip options. You may be tempted to do so because "you" know the customer's needs, and know, or think you know, the best solution. If you are a good salesperson, you will be often right, but let the customer find out himself what is good for him. By not exploring options, you deny the customer the right to participate in discovering the very best solution. By pushing too much your own solution you might face an unexpected resistance, which will be very hard to overcome.

Whilst doing so, never loose sight of the fact that you need to summarise needs, consequences and payoffs and verify them once again. Make sure you summarise the features and benefits. Do the same for the weak points but summarise these before the strong points as customers always retain the last stated points. So always start with the weak points and finish with the strong points. In doing so, stress the added value. A customer purchases on "perceived added value".

Meetings

Meetings are a must in a branch but, as we all know, they are time consuming. Call a meeting only when absolutely necessary. Make sure the relevant people are there. Plan your meetings so that you can make them shorter and more efficient. Circulate a memo before the meeting with the key points of discussion. You may establish a timetable per subject. However, make sure that in any event you take time to close the meeting efficiently and summarise what has been said and eventually decided upon. Avoid at all costs meeting again to discuss what had been discussed at the previous meetings but forgotten by all but a few who were present.

A well known timespan of attention by attendees is maximum 45 minutes. Most will already have drifted off before then. For that reason, use visual aides whenever possible.

The more planning goes into a meeting the more effective that meeting will be. Make sure you follow up! As usual, ask yourself what the consequences would be if you did not have that meeting. Think as an entrepreneur: always consider as many options as possible.

At the meetings, keep a low profile; if you chair the meeting encourage others to speak. Listen as much as you can. Encourage people to be candid and constructive. Whatever the facts are, they are the past. You can work on the future and the essential to reaching excellence is this drive to improve on whatever you are doing as individuals and as a team. Make sure, when you chair the meeting, to summarise regularly what has been said. Take notes so that a meaningful summary can be made at the end and a clear plan drawn up of the follow up actions with relevant responsibilities. Set yourself deadlines! Goals should contain a stretching element.

Minutes should be taken at all meetings. They should be clear, to the point, short and written up on the basis of notes taken at the meeting. They should be processed shortly after the meeting and promptly distributed.

Finally think about the cost of a meeting. Think like a true entrepreneur!

Reporting

Reporting should be an example of clarity. How? Remember you are selling. So, what is the situation, what is the problem, what information is needed to get to a conclusion and how is the subject to be followed up?

The challenge is to be brief. We worked for a bank where executive summaries for the board could not be longer than one A4 page. Before writing, do you have all the facts straight? You can only summarise what you master! You are marketing each time you write a memo. You are selling your image as well as your ideas and recommendations. So, what about the lay-out? Is the lay-out clear, pleasant? Are key points highlighted?

Once you have written something that pleases you, put it aside for a while and read it again before sending it out as if you were the person to whom that memo is addressed. Look at it critically. Is it clear or too complicated? Are your recommendations and expectations clear? How will the message be perceived? Best scenario, worst scenario? Do not expect people to agree automatically as there is a lot of competition out there. What is your fall back position?

Listening

It may seem strange that we list here the capacity to listen. You might think that this is quite obvious. Now, experience has shown that we are all poor listeners unless we consciously practice listening.

The factors which will prevent you from listening will be diverse and will be either the result of your own attitude or the result of external factors. Let us be generous and list a few external factors first:

✓ Distractions
✓ Interruptions
✓ Temperature
✓ The way you are seated
✓ Wandering thoughts
✓ Tiredness
✓ Monotone voice
✓ Jargon

Maybe you would like to list your own internal factors!

Learn to listen as it will be one of your major assets and in addition, it will save you a lot of time! It will also force you to be accurate, to the point, all things which are expected from a manager.

Training and coaching

The need for training shows an ever increasing trend. Unfortunately, the time available for training is gradually decreasing. Many organisations switch to self study during or outside working hours with compulsory exams or certifications. Most budgets have been spent on selling and the products.

In our experience, customers are generally unimpressed by the average employee and his or her lack of understanding of business.

In fact, every person working in a financial institution, whatever his position should have a basic knowledge of economics and finance. Luxembourg is a good example in this instance. Every employee, irrespective of their level of education, goes through a training program in banking. Obviously the levels differ but the modules are identical. Basically, there are three levels per module. The success story of Luxembourg is not a coincidence. The financial community of Luxembourg knows very well that its survival greatly depends on the training of every single individual working in the banking community.

So, in your branch training is essential and even more so if you have reduced your staff to a minimum. If everything else is too expensive or too difficult to implement, at the very least the best trainer in the branch should be the branch manager. Training widens the horizon of the employees, enhances their chances for a career development and is the best reward for top performance. And it contributes to the team spirit! In fact, by training your staff you literally become their coach. Every team needs a coach.

Training and coaching should be an ongoing process aimed at improving some aspects of an employee's or team's work performance. To be an effective coach as branch manager you need to establish mutual objectives and coach with those objectives in mind. Throughout the process, you offer support and help. Before that you will have created a team spirit, an environment in which your staff feel they can get guidance and assistance.

You will appreciate the following list of the principles of coaching:

♦ Demonstrate goal commitment and persistence in achieving the goals

♦ Help your staff develop plans to improve performance

♦ Communicate honestly and directly

♦ Be supportive and helpful in daily contacts

♦ Pay close attention to what your employees say

♦ Give feedback on performance

♦ Utilise recognition and rewards

We are sure that you will think that you have read this already. Of course this is very similar to performance measurement. The whole process is interrelated with this obsession of yours: "performance improvement". Consequently coaching is not an event, but an ongoing process.

There are differences between managing and coaching! It is not always easy to combine the two functions. As a coach you help people in achieving their own objectives. As a manager you make sure the branch's objectives are met. There should not be a conflict of interest but there might be. Coaching, training is helping, improving knowledge, whereas managing is making sure all is well in order to improve the performance as planned.

Coaching and training is an integral part of the day to day life of the branch and of the career development plan. It will help you in knowing your staff better as well as their potential. It will also ensure that the whole system operates in all fairness. For instance, it would not be logical that you would rate a person three (one being the best, five the worst) and recommend him for a promotion on the basis that he is exceptional in his current job and capable of continued growth.

---

3) The Forum Corporation, Effective selling

The potential of an employee is established day after day and your coaching is enabling this to be a pleasant and fair process. It goes hand in hand with motivation, communication, understanding, mutual respect, and all those other issues which are the ingredients of excellence.

It goes without saying that in order to succeed in this specific field of your responsibilities you need to set an example yourself. You need to have created a climate of confidence, of responsible relationships. You need to have had all the training you could get yourself before telling the others how and why they should be taking certain actions. We are back to the listening side of your profession as branch manager.

What can you do to motivate people if increased remuneration is not possible or is insufficient? Based on long experience, we strongly suggest: **M**anagement **B**y **O**bjectives (M.B.O.)

> Having covered your needs, now that you are succeeding let us see what you can do for your colleagues so that they can succeed as well.

Management by Objectives (M.B.O.)

The philosophy of management by objectives is that every employee has reached a recognised level of performance, from which he can, and should improve. Obviously, it entails that all employees have a **job description**. It is essential that there is no misunderstanding possible about the areas of responsibility. A job description can be factual or behavioural as shown by the example on the following page.

The next step is to determine what practical objectives need to be reached by this person in that specific job. Objectives should be mutually agreed, should be tangible, measurable and realistic. The employee may be stretched but his goals should be reasonable. Those objectives should be a part of the overall objectives of the branch.

Performance should be reviewed on a continuous basis. This means that in the case of none or weak performance the employee is counselled immediately. However, once a year the performance should be appraised in a more formal manner. Some banks even impose a quarterly formal review in line with the quarterly profit forecast. There should be no surprises as to the items discussed. The purpose of the review should not be an in depth analysis of the past but an assessment of attained objectives, of the present situation of the employee and above all **it should be forward looking**. **The goal is to improve on the present performance, whatever it is.**

Here you are! How can you go forward from here? How can you improve on what you are doing? Motivation will come from reaching objectives on the one hand, and from the assistance provided by the supervisor to the employee in order to reach this performance improvement, on the other.

MBO requires a fair and ethical attitude. Failures should be recognised and corrected and improvement rewarded. A person, who has reached his goals should be given a different job requiring new skills or a promotion in due time. The best performers should be selected for promotions in line with their proven skills. An additional benefit of the system is that promotions will be less influenced by in-house politics. This situation will create an atmosphere whereby the best, not the best connected, are promoted.

Here we come to the most powerful argument on motivation: "skills, know-how"! **You are what you know**. You will progress in corporate life because of what you have learned and continue to learn. You will progress because you contribute to the learning organisation. You will be motivated by your drive to improve on whatever you are doing and to know more. Status and financial reward will follow but they are not the strongest motivator.

How can you be sure the system works? By being fair, by rewarding those who really want to move forward and by penalising those who do not. It is a system whereby **you either move upwards or outwards** but where there is no room for mediocrity. Average performance pushes overall performance downwards. You want to move upwards, not downwards. The competition is out there to take your customer! If every single individual aims to move upwards, the organisation as such is moving upwards. The ultimate goal is to be seen to be better than the others. It is the responsibility of everybody, irrespective of that person's position in the organisation.

This system has to become an integral part of your **Corporate Values!** The essential element is: training, make sure staff learn as much as they can, even beyond their job so that they can prepare themselves and be up to the task when job rotation or promotion occurs.

Management Background

**An extract of an example of a behavioural job description
– Account Manager –**

Accountability

Knowledge of competitors and economy
Can discuss thoroughly:
✓ *Competition and location*
✓ *Primary products and services*
✓ *Major strengths and limitations*
✓ *Basis for pricing arrangements*
✓ *Economic trends and interest rates*

Knowledge of the bank's products

Can discuss accurately:
- ✓ *Features / characteristics of the consumer and Private Banking products*
- ✓ *Benefits of products and services relevant to the need of the client or prospect*
- ✓ *Benefits of the distribution channels*
- ✓ *Personal sales and service capabilities*

Follow-up

Is in a position to:
- ✓ *Keep commitments to customers and prospects*
- ✓ *Inform other business departments of details involved in handling specific transactions*
- ✓ *Update the account development and strategy*
- ✓ *Plan phone calls on a periodic level*
- ✓ *Ensure new producst are presented to prospects and customers*

Selling skills

- ✓ *Establishes a good rapport*
- ✓ *Makes appropriate introductions*
- ✓ *Discusses interests*
- ✓ *Adapts communications to the profile of the customer and prospect*
- ✓ *Exhibits listening skills*
- ✓ *Summarises needs which have been identified*
- ✓ *Tests understanding*

Performance evaluation

Here follows a table of content of an evaluation exercise[4].

1. Description of the tasks & responsibilities performed in the context of his/her professional activity in the bank during the year.

2. Skills required for the tasks

1. Training courses
2. General knowledge
3. Experience
4. Use of PC.
5. Languages
6. Others

3. Assessment of work performed

1. Technical and professional knowledge
2. Work ability
3. Performance of delegated work
4. Capacity to work without supervision
5. Efficiency and reliability
6. Professional conscientiousness
7. Initiative
8. Creativity
9. Character & co-operation
10. Attitude
11. Decision - making (Judgement)
12. Sense of responsibility
13. Emotional maturity
14. Communication skills
15. Animation skills
16. Company Integration
17. Other criteria

4. Objectives

1. Evaluation of objectives for previous year: Objectives 1 to 5
2. Objectives for next year
3. Measures to be implemented in order to achieve objectives
4. Additional training or experience required

5. How do you foresee your professional future development in the bank?

6. Global evaluation appraisal

7. Evaluator's comments

8. Evaluated comments

9. Final comments by the evaluator's superior

---

4) With the kind permission of a collegue banker.

The qualities of the evaluation process

Importance of the process

- ❑ The evaluation is to be considered as an important moment in an employee's career.
- ❑ It is the right time for a review!
- ❑ It is not primarily an evaluation, but the aim is to see if future expectations can be agreed upon and how performance can be enhanced.
- ❑ It is to be treated seriously. The evaluator has to take it very seriously. It is vital that sufficient time is devoted to the exercise.
- ❑ Preparation is important for both the evaluated and the evaluator.

Partnership

It has to be the basis for discussion

- ❑ It is the time to ensure that both parties know each other (especially for a new evaluator or evaluated).
- ❑ It enables both parties to receive feed-back from each other
- ❑ It is a joint discussion about future performance based on present performance
- ❑ The process should evolve into a habit of communication between the evaluator and the evaluated.

Respect

- ❑ Evaluator and Evaluated are both professionals and adults and have to act in that way.
- ❑ Even if tough things have to be said, the way they are expressed should remain professional.
- ❑ Avoid reactions based on emotions, and remain objective by having respect for the evaluated

❏ A warm attitude should be adopted throughout the process

❏ The interview should be fixed orally. The Evaluator should "invite" the Evaluated to the interview and

❏ not simply send, for instance, a cool e-mail

Constructive

❏ The term Evaluation is not the most appropriate to express the idea of this process, because it implies the notion of judgement. The Evaluator has to correct this image. We are not talking about a judgement but about ways to improve on performance.

❏ Both parties should keep in mind that the process must be constructive and conclude with solutions, goals and agreements

❏ In order to be as constructive as possible the preparation should be done by the Evaluated

❏ It is of paramount importance that it is a positive process for everyone. There is no "winner" and loser". The operation benefits the evaluated, the evaluator and the branch.

Objective

❏ Quantitative and identifiable measurements are essential for the objective setting

❏ Evaluators must avoid the "you have to improve" or "do your best" as objectives
   - Objectives are not "tasks"
   - The qualitative remarks are very important

❏ Problems are always of a "consultant type"; they are never "personal".

❏ You make sure the right person is in the right place

Specific

❏ Should be as precise as possible but with some flexibility

❏ They should be linked to the overall plan of the unit

❏ They should be crystal clear to the employee

❑ If need be, specify what resources will be allocated in order to reach the goal

❑ Set a time scale

❑ Comments of the employee should be carefully analysed when reviewing the goals, especially objections or reservations.

TIP: If you do not know what motivates a person, pursue it; discuss it.. If nothing really motivates the interviewed employee, encourage this person to work on it, if all else fails encourage this person to look for another employer!

Watch for behavioural patterns as far as motivation or absence of motivation is concerned. Check the level of motivation on an ongoing basis. Absenteeism due to a not very serious sickness, a faked depression, is quite often a warning that something is wrong.

Ratings in most corporations range from 1 to 5 with qualifications as insufficient, weak, average, good and very good. Salary increases are usually linked to performance measurement. Therefore, the ratings should be looked at conservatively otherwise the overall salary expenses will increase more than it logically should. Indeed, only about 5% to 10 % of employees are excellent with the vast majority as above average or average!

The person, who is negative or who is not willing to improve, drags down the overall performance of the branch. This is not acceptable. **Either an individual moves upward or outward**. Mediocrity will put the survival of all the branch members into jeopardy. Bear in mind, though, a few fundamental laws about performance as described in the box opposite this page.

No one said life is easy. Motivation is needed to acquire knowledge and achieve goals! Make sure your employees are aware of the competitive environment. **Train them in the basic principles of marketing. Make sure they know that their future is at stake.** Their job is not for ever. They could lose their job! Motivate them so that they are prepared to do the utmost to reach their objectives. Management means achieving this aim, which obviously starts with the branch manager!

So for the branch manager, the prerequisite for this process to function properly is setting yourself the goal to reach the ultimate. An old saying goes that the best motivation is the one which comes from the top and that is where you are!

> Tip: By the way, if you know that the meeting will be difficult for whatever reason, plan the meeting when your energy level is at its highest, which is often in the morning rather than late in the afternoon, when it is usually at its lowest. Take time; this is an important meeting for both of you. Run this meeting as professionally as you possibly can.

Finally make sure the employees have access at any time to at their evaluation forms. There should be no secrets here. The system is only credible if transparent.

Management Background

A-Z OF MANAGEMENT PRINCIPLES (Source FT)

The laws of Pareto, Parkinson and Peter

The idea that management is a science and therefore subject to fundamental laws has been around for at least 100 years. However, attempts to define a basic set of "Principles of management" have so far failed. Management is a human activity and therefore subject to cognitive bias and inconsistent behaviour; and further, the changing economic and social environment means that the demands on and needs of management are in a state of near-constant evolution. It is possible to construct any number of theories as to how management should be done in a perfect world, but the perfect world does not exist. Instead, rather than trying to work to "perfect" formulae, most of us do most things on an ad hoc basis. Some "Principles" that seem to have lasting validity have been developed: three of these are the Pareto Principle, Parkinson's Law and the Peter Principle.

The Pareto Principle,

Named after the economist Vilfredo Pareto, this principle was actually developed by the quality guru, Joseph Juran. Juran observed that most quality defects are attributable to a small number of causes, and termed this the phenomenon of the "vital few and the trivial many": it later became known as the "80-20 rule". Thus 80 per cent of quality defects come from problems with 20 per cent of processes; customers account for 80 per cent of revenue; 20 per cent of business units account for 80 per cent of production, and so on. Managers often take this to mean they should concentrate on the "vital few" and ignore the rest. However, there is a reduction ad absurdum here. We can get rid of the unprofitable 80 per cent of our customers and concentrate on the profitable 20 per cent; but if the principle really works, then 20 per cent of the remainder will in turn be "vital" and 80 per cent "trivial", and so on. There is no getting away from Pareto, so it is probably better to recognise it and work with it rather than try to beat it.

Parkinson's Law,

Formulated by the historian, C. Northcote Parkinson, states that "work expands to fill the time available". It is an essential characteristic of bureaucracies and hierarchies where rivalries develop between offices and departments. Bureaucrats inflate their workloads to perpetuate their own positions. Parkinson also observes that bureaucrats "multiply subordinates, not rivals", and measure their own importance by the number of juniors who report to them. Parkinson's Law is endemic; it contributes to the "silo" effect of strongly entrenched vertical hierarchies, which affects most large organisations at some point. Once they reach this stage, an expensive restructuring is usually the only solution.

The Peter Principle,

From the psychologist Laurence Peter, who states that "in a hierarchy, every employee tends to rise to the level of his own incompetence". Organisations promote employees to senior positions based on merit; but merit is measured on how well employees are carrying out their present jobs, not on how well they may carry out future jobs. This becomes a problem when, as is often the case, employees and managers are promoted into positions for which they are not suited. The "level of incompetence" has been reached; there is no further promotion and dissatisfaction of employee and employer is the result.

These Principles show how much of success - or failure - in management depends ultimately on the human factor and how difficult it is to construct perfect "systems" in management.

Morgen Witzel

I found a good definition of Management in an article in the Financial Times on Peter Drucker, the well known guru of management: "Management is neither a science nor an art, it is a practice of which results, and not academic degrees, are the measurement.

Goals

In any event, make clear that the organisation has high expectations. The corporate culture is to settle only for the best. You will see that people will try to live up to expectations, if they know their results will be recognised and rewarded. Don't be afraid of maintaining high expectations.

Persuade people to give the best of themselves on facts, not emotions. Take interest in what they are trying to achieve and listen to their difficulties. You are a manager, so it is your task to make sure they get there, if they try to! Therefore, make sure you listen carefully.

Learn to listen. It is not easy, especially if you are strong minded.

Rewarding

Staff are paid to do an excellent job, so their pay level should in principle be sufficient to match a very good performance. However, leave some leeway in your budget to reward "outstanding performance". Outstanding means really the best either in absolute or relative terms.

But first look at non salary increase rewarding, like, for instance, a membership of a health club or business club. Look at the participation in a savings- or pension- or training scheme. The individual might often value those rewards more than extra money, especially if the individual falls in a high tax bracket and knows that more than 50% of the salary increase will be taken away.

In our view the best reward remains training. Executive training in a prime Business School is beyond the means of most people. For instance, one week would easily carry a tuition fee of more than 7.000 Euro. A junior training course of several weeks would cost well over 15.000 Euro. The institution need not be so prestigious. A local university might be less well known but contribute appreciably to the know how of your staff.

Another good incentive, would be some training in one of the bank's branches abroad. If the bank has no branches, some training with one of its correspondent banks might achieve the same end.

In our part of the world there is an increasing tendency to award decent salaries and allow for a bonus on top which is performance related. It encourages employees to strive for top performance day after day. As we all know, in performance it is not just the level which matters but the continuity. The negative side of this system is that people concentrate so much on the coming bonus that they take decisions which could be to the detriment of the organisation in the long run.

It is worth considering setting up, at corporate level, a Master of Business incentive training program, whereby top performers, recommended by the branch or division managers, are sent on a MBA program. A condition to this would be that the employee stays with the organisation five years after his studies. If he leaves earlier, he must repay the tuition fees. Alternatively, why not finance the tuition at a subsidised rate? The employees could take a one or two year leave to study with a forgiveness of debt if they stay for at least five years after completion of the program.

What about extra pension contributions? What about stock options of the corporation?

If all this is not applicable, what about a membership of a social or sporting club? It is often the best place to find new customers. What about allowing some time to be invested in local community activities so that the branch is even more integrated into the local scene and broadens the customer base?

What would your employees think about a wine and cheese evening, an outing to a local pub on the branch's expense? You could even organise cocktails at the end of the afternoon with your customers and employees on the branch premises. If your branch is large enough, you might consider art exhibitions and serve some cocktails, always with the involvement of your staff. If you do this regularly, a team spirit will gradually build up.

Now, if all of this is not to your taste, why not rotate the top performer. Each job has specific requirements. If you give a successful person another job the chances that he will perform outstandingly will be great. On top of that, this person will have enlarged his or her field of expertise and this will allow for another more complex challenge in due time.

The ultimate reward obviously remains a well deserved promotion. For that very reason and because of the likelihood of their continued performance, it is the top performers who should be promoted. However, this does not mean that all can make it to the top, even if all would like to reach it. Certain jobs require certain well defined qualifications. Being a top performer does not necessarily equate to possessing the qualifications for another job. For instance, an outstanding salesperson is seldom an outstanding manager. Both jobs require intrinsically different qualifications and quite different personalities.

Promotions should be fair. The resentment of employees to unfair promotions is often underestimated and results in lack of respect and trust in senior management. Politics will always exist in branches and larger organisations but should be tolerated to the strict minimum and should really be played down at the decisional level. **The attitude should be – and this should be part of the Corporate Ethics: "Let the best win".**

In entities where this is not strictly adhered to, excellence is not at the end of the tunnel but negligence, errors, lack of motivation and ultimately loss of customer relationships. It is that simple!

Another way to motivate is to make sure that performance improvement is described and praised in the periodical newsletter of your bank or branch. When something outstanding happens, make sure it is known as it will benefit not just the individual involved but also others by means of example or by useful pieces of information for their own performance enhancement.

Dealing with tension

Not all discussions will be pleasant. You will probably face tension which is either goal related or personal conflict. Tension usually occurs between two individuals with opposing communication styles or with opposing views on certain specific issues. It is a big time eater, so watch out for it and deal with it immediately. If you do not, it will impact on your mood but even worse it might impact on the results of the branch and your career! It is damaging for productivity.

We are back to selling. First, ensure you are cerain what the situation and what the problem are. Make sure you have all information that is available and look for a solution. As manager you are entering into the most difficult type of selling. Therefore, step back. Look at it as a consultant. Do not take it personally. You are here to solve a problem. Observe. It is the moment to take note of body language. Listen.

Do not make statements! The employee might seize it as a way to disagree with you and some people love to disagree just for the stake of it. Ask questions. There are no stupid questions, there are only stupid answers!

Get a conflict out of the branch. It is an absolute must. If you can not do it, ask a third party to do it, someone from the personnel department, for instance. Do not ask your boss to do it as you are supposed to alleviate his problems, not add to them!

If everything fails try to persuade the person that his or her numerous talents would come to fruition in a place other than the branch.

Thinking as a matter of fact

You may remember that in the seventies IBM made the decision to put on every officer's desk a little desk-plate with the word:"Think". Indeed, IBM thought it could guarantee its survival through all its responsible officers and employees permanently "thinking" about what they were doing and why. Today IBM is still successful and in fact an increasing portion of its revenues comes from systems consulting rather than manufacturing.

Encouraging people to think helps them in gaining this shared sense of responsibility, which you need in order to move towards reaching your objectives. Encourage people to speak out constructively. The only welcome criticism is constructive criticism. Ask your employees often what they would do when confronted with an issue. Always encourage people to give the best of themselves.

At Bank of America, years ago the bank started a "thinking program". The goal was to make recommendations to the bank on all sorts of issues with a view to reducing cost. Most ideas came from what was called the 'operations' part of the bank. When a suggestion had been implemented, the bank calculated the added value and the relative cost reduction and shared 10% thereof with the employee who had generated the idea.

Remember the statement one makes about marketing. Marketing is a methodology, a way of thinking. Thinking in marketing terms or in cost reduction terms or in performance enhancement terms or in entrepreneurial terms should be part of the culture of your organisation and hence of your branch!

Creative thinking is the responsibility of all! This will only be achieved through team building. Encourage brainstorming sessions, where all ideas are welcome as long as they are constructive. Always keep in mind this obsession, which is to improve the performance of the branch. Let ideas flow freely.

Delegation

Delegation is a good way to motivate people. It means: "I trust you". It means: "these objectives are in good hands". Delegation is as key to the employee as it is to you. It will help you in managing your time better and it will help the employee in gaining much needed know-how to progress in the organisation. Really, from a manager's point of view, you should have employees, who are so motivated and knowledgeable that you can delegate most of your duties. **The saying goes: "work yourself out of your job" so that you can move on.** Delegation will also make people more responsible and gradually make them think like entrepreneurs.

First, try to make a list of everything you are doing and ask if some tasks are really relevant. Of those which are, which ones could be dealt with by others and which ones could only be dealt with by you alone? Retain the latter and concentrate on those. Delegate all the others.

Consider all the facts before delegating. Monitor on an ongoing basis and ensure that your support is there initially. Allow errors only at the beginning! We are back to the main source of motivation: "know how". Make sure the person to whom you delegate has the required know how. If this is not entirely the case arrange training. Help the person to improve his or her skills. Help the person to progress and you will have a motivated employee working with you.

Set deadlines. Time always passes too quickly. Force yourself and your associates to meet strict deadlines! If a deadline is missed, ask yourself why this is the case and what could be done next time to improve on the present performance. Think like an entrepreneur and teach the others to think likewise. It is a struggle against time as invoices always come in faster than income!

If you think you cannot delegate a specific task to an individual because he is not trustworthy despite adequate training, talk about it and review the situation at performance evaluation. If you still think the same way offer another job to that person. Then, if you are still of the same opinion, you should consider a more radical solution based on a mutual understanding that a top performance will never be reached.

Delegation will also help you in making sure you have the right people in the right place. True there are some drawbacks in delegating but generally speaking they do not outweigh the advantages which are usually quite clear, such as motivation, competence improvement, gaining time. The disadvantages are initially time consumption, less control, needs negotiation, risk of non performance, risk of missing deadlines, lack of sense of detail. However, despite all this it will enable you to concentrate more on the expectations of your job as well as on yourself and your next step in the organisation.

Even when you have delegated a task it remains your responsibility! You could never use it as an excuse to justify a problem or a failure to your own boss. So, control and audit remains essential in order to protect yourself and your branch.

Team spirit

The ability to lead others is an essential feature of your job. Therefore you should gradually arrive at a position where **you stimulate people to be at their best and to use their initiative to achieve the goals of the branch**. It goes without saying that to get the best out of your staff you must set the example. To a certain extent employees need to admire the person who is leading them. They expect you to be competent whilst at the same time attentive to their needs and comments.

You have to rely on the strengths of your employees and delegate accordingly so that you can function as a manager rather than as the chief of a fire brigade. Obviously reaching this goal requires the co-operation of your employees. We are back to the MBO approach, i.e. you have to ask yourself what you can do for them so that they can improve their performance.

Be aware that your image is an important contributor to reaching your goal. For instance, if your office is a mess, what happens to the image and consequently the order and tidiness in the branch? Excellence is a sum of small details, which should be checked day after day. So the team spirit starts with your attitude.

For instance, a question you can ask yourself is: "Do I strive to achieve a positive atmosphere, in which people compete with ideas rather than with politics? " "Do I listen, do I really listen? " If you do, you will improve your career prospects! Listening is particularly important because all people think in a different way.

Think about the fact that managing is like selling. The key to selling is listening and competence. Agreed! you also need continuity and a bit of luck.

To attain a cohesive team spirit requires you to ensure that everyone is working towards the same goal. Criticise constructively. Praise and sanction when needed. Develop individual and team skills and train as much as you can. A good way to achieve this is brainstorming sessions where people talk freely. Make sure you collect contributions from everybody. Encourage team members to take part in the discussions. Each member may have something to add to the meeting. Make sure they are firmly committed to contributing to the meeting and implementing decisions taken. We are back to selling here! What is the situation, what is the problem, what is the information needed to come to a conclusion!

When you meet objections, which prevent you from working as a team, look at the rationale. Leave the emotions aside. Always look at things in a positive manner and ask questions. Consider all the options before losing the goodwill of valued team members. Never loose sight of the fact that members must be supportive of each other. They share the same interest and should reach the same goal. Therefore, teams, like individuals, should have clear goals. In small branches the sum of all the goals of the employees and the manager would be the objectives of the branch as such.

An added value of the team is that people will learn from each other. You are what you know! A team should contribute to its overall know how and therefore enhance the team members' career prospects.

> A tip: in a team every member is equally important and the position in the structure of the unit is irrelevant!
>
> Be particularly aware of problems as they affect the overall performance of the branch (and your career!). Follow up.

Being a cohesive team up has become even more of an issue since branches have moved towards retail outfits. When there is face to face interaction with the customer working life becomes more intense and a weak performance of one person will necessarily affect the performance of the whole team! Many retail financial organisations still have a long way to go in that respect. It is matter of motivation, training, culture and corporate spirit.

---

5) For further reference : Robert Heller in "Achieving excellence", Dorling Kindersley, London, ISBN 0.7513.0768.8

Pursuing excellence

It is a matter of attitude, of mentality. Never be satisfied with something which is less than perfect. Therefore, be your first and own critic. Day after day, ask how you can improve. Look continuously at what you are doing and how. Ask yourself what can be changed so that your branch becomes more efficient. Listen to comments, which might help you in enhancing whatever can be improved. Everything matters in this instance. Constantly seek to improve your performance by setting new and higher targets for yourself. Take every opportunity to learn and exercise new skills.

How do you make your decisions? In a truly professional way or intuitively, based on assumed facts or on hearsay? Have you looked at the alternatives? Are you afraid of changing your decisions if an alternative proves more effective? How do you consider the implications of your decisions on the employees, on the results of the branch? Are you really taking time to consider what might go wrong? Are those decisions in line with the overall objectives of the bank, the branch and your own career?

Are you too intuitive? Did you really analyse the situation and listen to what others had to say about it? You have many skills and know how. Did you use them when making a decision?

Would you take chances with your own money? Think of the net worth of the branch as your own net worth (the difference between the assets and the liabilities to third parties). Think like an entrepreneur again. Wrong decisions affect your business and the careers of your staff and the survival of all of you.

Do not try to mix politics with business decisions! Decisions are good because they will enhance the profitability of the branch or alternatively enhance motivation or team building. Therefore encourage your staff to put ideas forward, which might lead to shared, understood decisions.

A little tip! When you are angry or stressed: do not make decisions on the spot. You might regret it later. Wait, listen, analyse, look at the alternatives and than make a decision. Be aware of the effect of your decisions on the employees.

We class problem solving under the sales process, because problem situations are special cases, where you will need all your selling skills.

Another little tip! Do not forget cultural differences. In the EU, we gradually moved away from the old hierarchical or order and obey system and replaced it with a consensual way of working.

Marketing

Let us take a quick look at the marketing environment of the financial services industry as it impacts on the situation of your branch.

The evolution in the banking industry

1970-1980

The seventies were characterised by a deep change in competition within the banking industry from internationalisation, predominantly caused by competition from large US banks, often called the money centre banks. The expansion of US banks was restricted to their home state and they therefore sought to expand abroad.

1980-1990

The eighties saw the banks split into retail banks, merchant banks, investment banks and so-called private banks. This drastic change implied a better segmentation of the customer base, an increased specialisation, and large investments in systems and in people. The retail banks specialised in the mass distribution of financial products. The merchant banks specialised in the financing of commercial and financial transactions; the investment banks in the issuance of stocks and bonds; the so-called private banks in wealth management.

1990-2000

The nineties saw the introduction of electronic systems but above all increased competition from non-banks: the fund managers, the retailers, and the software houses, not to mention the insurance companies. Today the big competitors of banks are not other banks but the distributors of products and information.

2000-2010

This decade will witness ever increasing competition and a marked split between the multinational financial service institutions and the niche players. In any event, the survival of each will depend on the quality of their products and their services. Survival will depend upon the permanent search for excellence, hence the significance of management and in particular branch management. We have noticed over recent years that the significance of the branch has changed but not really diminished. In addition, bankers will increasingly become retailers.

Roughly, the evolution of the banking industry forces the banks to face four major challenges:

❑ *The marketing challenge*
❑ *The distribution challenge*
❑ *The risk management challenge*
❑ *The human challenge*

The marketing challenge

A financial institution needs a distinct image to differentiate it from other financial institutions. This unique image needs to be clear in the minds of the consumers, the prospects but also in the minds of the employees and the shareholders. The very survival of the institution is being threatened by competition from distributors and by the technical revolution. In order to survive, the institution needs to be perceived as better and different from the others. There is no choice but to search for excellence!

Excellence must be everyone's goal. The institution's reputation is its main asset. The above-mentioned changes, when combined with increased revenues and wealth, an expanding economy and a clear globalisation of the financial services, have generated a particularly competitive environment for the industry dominated by an ever increasing sophisticated demand from consumers.

The distribution challenge

The ATM (Automated Teller Machine) has led the way to the automation of various financial transactions. They have been introduced after a long overdue cost analysis of the networks of branches. **Furthermore, one should not fail to notice that today one can purchase most banking products without using a bank.**

Since the early eighties, non financial institutions (predominantly fund managers and insurance companies) have been authorised to offer to the public a large choice of financial products. In addition, most of those institutions had lower costs because of the absence of a branch network and better trained specialists for certain more sophisticated products.

The banking industry is at a crossroads. The nature of the competition changes!

Technology increases competition and productivity; however it does not bind customers to the institutions. The challenge is a tough one. It increasingly boils down to a software challenge linked with quality of service and value as perceived by consumers.

The challenge of risk management

There are many risks inherent to the financial services. The essential ones are relative to:

❑ Foreign Exchange: The markets exchange daily over 1.5 billion Euro; this volume is disconnected from the real economy, the exchange rates therefore become quite unpredictable

❑ Transfer: The counterpart cannot transfer the money as agreed due to, for example, a credit squeeze.

❑ Capital Markets: Who would pretend that the future would be a linear extrapolation of the past?

❑ Credit: The economic cycles are often characterised by either a surplus of credit or a credit squeeze.

❑ Reputation: The market recognises excellence promptly but brutally penalises mediocrity.

❑ Interest rates: The banking environment is eminently sensitive to the fluctuation of interest rates. This is equally valid for investments in securities.

The human challenge

Life has become much more demanding in the financial services industry. Years ago it was a matter of selling a few products to un-segmented customers by means of the branch. Today there is a broad range of financial products including investment and insurance products. The required know-how in this field is highly technical. Furthermore these products are being sold to segmented customers through a wide variety of distribution channels.

All this requires employees of a different type. Even more so because employers are shifting a larger part of the responsibility for success towards employees, who are increasingly regarded as consultants, i.e. on a job performance basis. Employees are therefore under increased pressure to perform in order to retain their jobs.

Added to this new environment is the problem of adequately understanding consumer needs and desires and projecting consumer behaviour relative to new products and services as well as the changing pattern in the area of electronic distribution systems.

Finances involve very basic human needs and emotions in respect of protection, security and control. When it comes to handling or managing their finances, particularly where more complex decisions or larger sums of money are involved, most customers consider personal service and expertise to be important. This puts an additional pressure on branch management and the employees.

Additionally, banks see ever increasing competition from non-industry related providers of financial services. The burden is on the banks. "Alternative providers are not bringing any great competitive advantage to the table; so long as banks continually re-engineer the processes so that they are efficient, so long as banks continually adapt to the most worthwhile innovations, so long as banks continually put the customer first[6].

> *Above all, financial institutions need to recognise that to be successful they must focus sharply on their most precious asset: their customers.*

6) J. Svigals, "Distribution 2000", Lafferty publications, 1996

Marketing as a way of thinking

Marketing is not the exclusive responsibility of the marketing department but of every single person working for an organisation. Every employee is the company's ambassador. Management has, in this field, a compounded responsibility.

Generally speaking marketing is a methodology, which structures the way people think of sales or advertising or other related considerations. However it is much more than that. **Marketing is a way of thinking**, a way of analysing, of asking questions, the right questions! Therefore a basic knowledge of marketing is a must for "all" employees.

As branch manager, it goes without saying that you are familiar with the marketing environment. However, do not assume the same of your team. Therefore, make sure their knowledge is at the optimum level in this field.

The ultimate goal of marketing is to be seen to be different and better than the competition. This can only be achieved through the close involvement of all concerned. There is no difference in this field between management and staff. All need to be performance driven and share the same goals.

Surprisingly, in the banking industry marketing is a "relatively" recent business philosophy. Banks have always been in a somewhat privileged position and could afford not to be customer oriented. Compared with other industries, retail banks have paid less attention to consumer needs and desires. Companies in the packaged goods, consumer electronics, software or automobile industries have much better records in this area.

There are various reasons for this situation: historical, cultural, but most probably the fact that banks did not need to be market driven because of the emphasis on control, caution and risk avoidance which did not encourage innovation, market research and testing. Times have changed:

*Multiple forces are affecting the financial services industry: over-capacity, high-cost structures, new technologies, changing consumer behaviour and expectations, competition. **Even the pace of change is changing.***

Management Background

Marketing in a nutshell

Any book on marketing will quickly reach about 750 pages. The structure of marketing discipline is about this:

- 📖 **Basic Concepts of Marketing:** *general Principles, marketing challenges, the marketing environment and strategic planning*

- 📖 **Marketing Opportunities:** *marketing research and information systems, influences on consumer behaviour and buyer decision processes*

- 📖 **Market Segmentation:** *defining the market, measuring current market demand, market segmentation for a competitive advantage.*

- 📖 **Market Mix:** *designing products, product life cycle strategies, pricing, distribution channels, placing products, promoting products, advertising & public relations,*

- 📖 **Creating a Competitive Advantage:** *quality, value and service, a competitive analysis*

Most key marketing issues would be covered not at branch level but at headquarter's level. However marketing is a top down and bottom up process. The best source of information is the employees who face the daily requirements of the customers; hence they are well placed to transmit their demands. It is therefore essential that your employees are familiar with the basic concepts of marketing, which we have summarised for ready reference.

The best source of marketing information is the employees. They face customers on a daily basis and are confronted with routine requirements. It is essential, even if you think that this might be a waste of time, to transmit information to the central marketing unit. Moreover, if all units transmit information systematically the central unit will have but one choice, which is to take your recommendations into account.

Don't be afraid to use humorous factual examples to demonstrate your point. For instance: You find you have a great product from a technical point of view but for which the presentation is dismal. Ask the marketing officer if he had a choice between a nicely wrapped packet and a poorly wrapped one, which he would select. He would certainly take the nicely wrapped package. Ask him then why the product is so poorly wrapped.

Basic Principles of marketing [7]

Selling is only the tip of the iceberg, *it is only one of many marketing functions. The aim of marketing is to know and understand the customer so well that the product or service fits… and sells itself .*

People satisfy their needs and desires with products. People have almost unlimited desires but limited resources. Thus people choose that which provides the most satisfaction for their money.

*The buying pattern is based on **their perceptions of a product's value**. The guiding concept is **customer value**.*

The concept of product is not limited to physical objects. The importance of products is not so much in owning them as in the benefits they provide. Consumers face a broad array of products. Research about how consumers form value judgements and make product choices is a key to success.

*A market occurs when people decide to satisfy their needs and desires through **exchange**. Money still plays a key role as an instrument for exchange. Whereas exchange is a core concept of marketing, a **transaction** is marketing's unit of measurement. A **transaction** consists of a trade of values between two parties.*

---

7)   P. Kotler and G. Armstrong : " Principles of Marketing", Prentice Hall, New Jersey 1994

*Transaction marketing is part of a larger idea of **relationship marketing.** Successful marketing builds a long-term relationship with valued customers with consistency, high quality and excellent service and fair pricing, i.e. by maximising mutually beneficial relationships. The concept of transactions leads to the concept of a **market**. A market is a set of actual and potential transactions of products.*

There are various markets. Amongst others, the money market is an important market that meets people's needs so that they can borrow and invest money in the short term. The capital market would be that vehicle for transactions over one year. The foreign exchange market would be a market where currencies are being exchanged for other currencies, for example US dollars sold in order to acquire Euro.

***Marketing means analysing and working in markets, to bring about exchanges for the purpose of satisfying human needs and desires** Sellers must search for buyers, identify their needs, design appropriate products, promote them, store and deliver these products and set prices for them. Activities such as product development, research, communication, distribution, pricing and service are core marketing activities.*

***Marketing management is** the analysis, the planning, the implementation, the control of programs designed to create, build, and maintain beneficial exchanges with target customers for the purpose of achieving organisational objectives; **and therefore covers:** sales, advertising, promotion, research, product development, pricing research, and others.*

*The **marketing concept** implies that achieving organisational goals depends on determining the needs and wants of target markets and delivering the desired satisfaction more effectively and efficiently than competitors do.*

*Banks should look at **future customer needs and wants** and their usage of services and distribution channels in order to develop an effective, long-term integrated marketing concept.*

Basic Principles of strategic planning

***The hard task of selecting an overall company strategy for survival and growth is called strategic planning.** The basic mission should be a source of deep strength providing some overall distinctive competence which can be built upon for the development of future* *strategy. Thus, a concept of the overall direction the institution wishes to pursue needs to be identified and the nature of the activities it will engage in as well as self-imposed constraints that may apply as a result of history, culture and management values.*

Marketing plays an important role in strategic planning. It provides information and other inputs to plan. In turn, strategic planning defines marketing's role in the organisation. Planning forces management to think ahead systematically. It forces the company to sharpen its objectives and policies, leads to better co-ordination of company efforts, and provides clear performance standards. In a fast changing environment planning is even more essential as it helps the company to anticipate and respond quickly to environmental changes and face sudden developments.

*Planning stems from the fact an organisation needs a clear purpose or **mission**.*

↓

*The company's mission needs to be turned into detailed supporting **objectives***

↓

*This leads to portfolio analysis and the definition of strategic **business units***

↓

*In addition, marketing strategies begin with a thorough competitor analysis. A strategy should lead at a point in time to a **competitive advantage**.*

↓

*Once the company has decided on its overall competitive marketing strategy it is ready to begin the details of the **marketing mix**.*

*The **marketing mix** is one of the major concepts. **Marketing Mix is defined as the set of controllable, tactical marketing tools that the company blends to produce the response it seeks in the target market**. The marketing mix consists of everything the company can do to influence the demand for its product. The many possibilities can be collected into four groups of variables known as the "four*

P's" : product, price, place and promotion. *Fortunately marketing specialists now recognise the need to add a fifth "P" for people. Indeed, they make the difference.*

The plan review presents an opportunity to evaluate the strategy chosen for a particular market. It also helps to provide feedback to market segment managers and give additional insights into the thinking behind the development of unit strategy. This is a constructive opportunity for **two-way feed back and communication.**

It should be clear that Corporate strategy deals with the development of an organisation's business activities, while marketing strategy focuses specifically on the organisation's activities in relation to the markets served.

As a business function, marketing has tended to play a largely tactical role. This has now changed for the better in the banking industry and marketing is now part of an integral organisational strategy and resulting market driven strategies. **Strategy is not just about being efficient; it is crucially concerned with enabling the organisation to be effective.**

The efficiency component simply relates to doing the task well, the effectiveness component relates to doing the right task, i.e. having the right products in the right markets at the most appropriate times. Thus, for example, from the perspective of a bank, strategy goes beyond simply ensuring that money transmission activities are performed in the most cost-effective manner; it requires that the bank is supplying the right type of money transmission facility, that which best meets the needs of the bank's customers. The organisation can only be effective if it is aware and responsive to the environment in which it operates.

Marketing planning implies effectiveness, efficiency, responsiveness & awareness of environmental changes.

In summary developing a fully integrated marketing infor-mation plan requires, at least:

❑ *a statement of objectives; which must be achievable, consistent and quantifiable*

❑ *an assessment of how the organisation is to develop its business in relation to its particular markets and on which segments to focus its attention*
❑ *determine the appropriate level of marketing expenditure*
❑ *develop the appropriate level of marketing mix*
❑ *the identification of specific tasks*
❑ *the allocation of those tasks to individuals*
❑ *the establishment of a monitoring system*
❑ *the implementation of procedures*
❑ *some elements of contingency planning*
❑ *permanent adaptation to changing circumstances*

The market focus has changed. Customers are increasingly recognised, because of the fast changing technological ways of communication, as individuals, no longer as segments. Banks will have to meet demand for personalised services and products that meet specific needs, and in doing so add more value than the competition.

Even if weaknesses and threats are not clearly perceived by the company they usually are by consumers.

This process might often lead to completely new strategies. A more balanced approach is an analysis based on market attractiveness and business strength. In any event, in a period of environmental turbulence it is becoming increasingly important to recognise that strategies need to be reviewed and adjusted as often as changes are being perceived in the market place; be it for products, competitors, whatever impacts the business.....Alertness to change is certainly the key to good planning.

The process of bank strategic planning is a vital ingredient in the development of systematic strategic management at all levels of the bank. The plan itself should be developed to become an important working document of management. However, it is only a framework for action; it is not and never can be a substitute for initiative, drive and creativity.

Marketing at Branch level

Successful implementation for strategic planning and marketing requires that certain conditions are met at branch level, i.e.:

a recognised need; there must be a clear and unequivocal recognised need that attention should be paid to the forward direction of the branch.

Unfortunately, this need often comes through "unsatisfactory" performance or competitive pressures, or sudden and unplanned serious loss,...

a leadership commitment; in part, planning may be seen as an element of   determining the movements in culture and strategic directions of the branch.

a suitable (re)organisation

the development of an Information Base on :
- market identification
- market segmentation
- market attractiveness measurement
- competitive position measurement
- business/customer/product profitability analysis
- strategic resource requirements assessment (human, systems and financial)
- control system design
- reward system development
- organisational change

a suitable control system design; the assessment of risk is usually the weak spot in this whole exercise. Heavy losses occur as a result of individuals rushing into a fashionable marketplace and in so doing abandoning strict credit assessment procedures.

reward and sanction system;

good communications to avoid inconsistencies and to overcome the ultimate inertia that tends to exist in most organisations; they act as a positive motivating force. They are necessary in isolating and reducing any potential resistance

time, sufficient time should be given to the process in order to permit good quality, acceptability and usage in the branch

Experience shows that it takes quite a few years before a planning system settles down and begins to produce meaningful results.

A company's **marketing environment** consists of factors and forces outside marketing that affect marketing management's ability to develop and maintain successful transactions with its target customers.

The future looks uncertain. A financial institution will have to strive for a lasting advantage; it will have to rely at branch level on:

❑ **Detailed knowledge of its customers** to provide a range of products and services that meet the needs of both individuals and businesses, large and small.

❑ **Developing into a learning and changing organisation** capable of responding quickly to changing needs.

❑ **Providing a clear communication** of vision to customers and employees.

❑ **Being an organised branch** with current employees being requested to master sets of new skills.

❑ **Increasing the usage of distribution systems,** e.g. increase ATM usage, phone banking, home banking

---

Detailed knowledge of the customer

Understanding how people are motivated to buy helps to:

- identify future customer needs more effectively
- improve the ability to communicate with potential customers
- emphasise the features of the services which might have the most appeal
- plan the marketing strategy to produce the desired results
- obtain the confidence of clients

Changing technology and the development of alternative delivery systems are providing a growing choice of possibilities to customers, making an understanding of customer behaviour even more important. Income and wealth affect the individual's need for credit or savings products. Personal factors, in particular the lifestyle and life-cycle stages, may affect the demand for mortgage and insurance products.

Psychological factors such as attitudes to risk, attitudes to debt and need for security, affect the extent to which different consumers perceive a need for a range of financial services.

The ideal opportunity to get to know a customer is when he is applying for a loan. He needs the money and will only be too happy to answer your questions and let you set up a data base. You can indeed draw the conclusion that in order to know your customer you should sell that type of product. Even a credit card would do the trick!

Once you have asked all the questions relative to the loan application you should already know which additional product you are going to sell!

Your proposal for a new product should be done before or after signature of the contract but in any event before the funds are transferred in his favour. Indeed you can be sure the customer will listen to you as long as his account has not been credited with the amount of the loan.

The best product to reach that goal is a mortgage loan. You will not only have all the information you need but also be in a position to keep a link with the customer for many years. It is an ideal marketing situation.

Often, when looking for information, we have a tendency to look well beyond the serving area of the branch. Use your employees' know how. If they are not as yet a good source of information, train them. In addition look at what the competition is doing. Maintain accounts with other institutions; see what they offer, how their brochures are designed, how their account statements are set out. Make a regular assessment of what your competitors do and offer.

A way of doing this is to ask a new staff member to visit the branches in the neighbourhood of your branch or the branches from your village and to inquire on products and services. Alternatively, you could have this done by a student working in the branch for a while.

It is easier said than done to be seen to be different and better than the others but it certainly starts with yourself as branch manager and with your staff as your associates in this adventure.

> The ideal moment to collect as much information as feasible is the opening-form for a current account.

The current account form should contain two major parts: one section should contain all the legally required information, such as prescribed by law, in the framework for instance of the prevention of money laundering, the other part should contain as much marketing information as the customer is willing to consider. Now, at the moment of the opening of the account the customers are usually willing to go that extra mile.

Make sure you know how and when to use this information. Remember the key to success is to be seen to be different and better than the others. How long ago did you get a birthday card from your branch manager, dear customer? How long ago did you get a personal call telling you that some of your money might be better invested than laying idle on a current account? How long ago did you get a call about insurance or a new product?

In a nutshell, know what business the customer conducts with the branch: make sure you keep track of the development of the relationship on file to assure continuity, be proactive, search for selling opportunities whilst you are building a long lasting relationship.

Investments as an example of gaining customer knowledge

Undeniably, one of the initial questions most customers will ask, even before a salesperson or financial advisor has a chance to analyse their goals, is: "How shall I invest my money?"

You have no chance of providing your customer with a meaningful answer unless you raise quite a lot of questions yourself.

Did you ever really watch a doctor?

Would he prescribe any drugs without taking the time to analyse the situation properly? Would you trust him, if he did? Investing is a less dramatic topic than health, but likewise, it does need time and careful attention. Rushing to the solution in this instance would be equally unwise.

The salesperson or the financial advisor would have to raise "at least" the following questions to be in a position to give a meaningful answer:

- What are the needs and the objectives?
- What are the requirements for liquidity?
- What is the objective as to return?
- What is the attitude vis-à-vis risk?
- What is the experience as far as investments are concerned?
- What is the base currency?
- What is the equity base?
- What is the time horizon of the investment?

You might wonder why one should ask 'at least" all those questions. Well, as a private investor, there is no reason to act differently than a professional investor. The objectives of the investor can be different but the approach must be the same. Moreover, one should never neglect to protect oneself from the market risk which is much more easily said than done.

The first question is thus a question of goals. In the USA, about half of the people invest for their retirement and an additional large number in order to face unforeseen events. Of course, there are quite a lot of other objectives, such as the purchase of a house, to protect oneself from inflation, medical expenses, the cost of higher education, etc.

An average customer, who would be drawing up a small list of his basic financial related characteristics, would certainly cover the following points:

- Income
- Household expenses
- Age
- Family structure
- His need, or lack of need, for liquidity
- His perception, or lack of perception, of inflation and interest rates
- His experience, or lack of experience, of the markets
- His tax situation
- His apprehension concerning the future; think of state pensions
- His apprehension concerning his life and security
- Apprehensions concerning the end of a career, a loss of earned income, etc.

The banker in this instance needs to be like a house doctor: know the patient well so that he can prescribe the right drug.

A good investment strategy will cover all these points as much as possible. A compromise will be a prerequisite. Everyone desires an exceptional profitability with low risk. It is not possible.

It is obvious that the better the customer is being profiled; the least risk is taken in presenting the most adequate product. In principle the purchase of any given investment product may be considered as a natural conclusion to the process of evaluation and profiling. However adverse publicity concerning the company or the product's performance may induce the customer to change his decision at the last minute. Showing a clear track record is the best argument in order to avoid last minute switches.

Needless to say, post purchase behaviour is likewise significant. Indeed, satisfaction will provide the basis for brand loyalty, at least brand awareness and establishment, and will provide the best possible advertising, i.e. favourable information to other potential customers[8].

Heavy users of financial products and risk takers, who are usually quite knowledgeable about financial markets, are found to be quite sensitive to economic and convenience factors.

To attract and retain customers the following are required:

- attractive pricing
- reliability
- flexibility
- quality
- professional follow up

Their loyalty should not be taken for granted.

8) "Marketing of financial services", C. Ennew, T. Watkins & M. Wright, Oxford

Developing into a learning branch ready for change

A learning branch

Excellence in today's market place demands more than a thorough knowledge of products. In an ever changing environment, every single day seems a new challenge. The macro- as well as the micro environment is changing quickly, maybe even too fast for a lot of customers and bank employees alike. The answer to this stress is to learn.

The first step is a marketing step. What are your strengths and weaknesses? Do things the easy way. Start playing on the branch's strengths and waste no time in rectifying your weaknesses. Listen to your employees and accept their critical comments.

However look at yourself, the branch manager, first. What are your strengths and weaknesses? What about your ambition, confidence, ability to take risks, drive, self-criticism, leadership? Can you mobilise to achieve group ambitions, as well as develop other employees and bring them forward? Can you work yourself out of your job? Can you move on? In other words, can you, teach, or inspire, others to reach their level of excellence?

> *How can you as branch manager transform the branch into a learning environment?*

First, take control. Lead your own team. Gain experience through expanding your leadership skills. Broaden your skills. Second, remember that the sum of the performances of all your employees is the basis of your success. Therefore, allow your subordinates to take positions that will widen their knowledge, their experience and above all, make sure they study for further qualifications that will assist them and yourself in reaching their goals.

You have to manage people to the extent that they are motivated to acquire the knowledge, experience, skills needed for advancement in the shortest possible time. That is why your employees have to have targets for both achievement and career moves. For that reason you need management by objectives which we will cover later.

Here again the marketing methodology is of help. Do research and avoid taking actions before you have all the facts. When one goal is achieved, set a new, higher one. Always seize an opportunity to delegate tasks.

> *Remember that leaders are only as good as those they lead.*

A learning branch is a branch where new skills are being acquired that are not linked to immediate work demands. Encourage people in thinking sessions to give full rein to their intuition as well as their logic. Take the lead, get other people to follow you when you start. In order to do that, you need to know more, not less than most of your employees!

What about "you" giving some training sessions? This would enhance your image and respect for your know-how and it would allow you to work at the same time on the issues of motivation, team spirit, productivity and so many other goals which you need to achieve.

A branch ready for change

The financial services industry is changing at great speed. The branch has to adapt to the new challenges under the guidance of the branch manager. Managing change is probably at the top of the list of responsibilities. It is easier said than done, especially given that in general people hate change. They resist change. Therefore the first task will be to determine what needs to be changed (remember your obsession is excellence). Convince people of the need to change and overcome their resistance, as well as ascertaining that implementation is effective.

A change is a challenge, is an opportunity to achieve a higher performance, therefore look for change. Welcome any comment of your associates which might change the branch for the better and allow for improved results. Whatever the suggestions for change from inside or outside sources may be, always consider them. It does not mean they can or should be implemented, but they will help you to "think". If someone in the branch is paid to think, you are!

A learning branch and a changing branch are really two sides of the same coin. It makes the whole operation more challenging, more interesting and more motivating. Obviously, change for the sake of it is not a good strategy as it might disrupt more than anything else the smooth way your branch is running, but it should never be far away.

You will encounter problems or even severe problems in the course of action. They are the opportunities forced upon you for change. Learn from problems in order to structure the future in an optimal way.

The most pleasant and motivating change is of course through growth. Growth not only forces people to adjust permanently and cope with increasingly demanding and complex jobs, but it is particularly motivating to "have the wind in the sails". It gets the best out of people.

> *Question yourself about change. What is going to change in the very near future? How is it going to impact my branch, the branch's performance, mine?*

Remember, only changes which give you a hedge versus other branches, or other colleagues or the competition are worth considering. Involve all of your staff. This is your branch. This is your future. Be particularly attentive to underlying reasons for resistance to recognised needs for change. Positivism, a constructive attitude is expected from your staff. Should this not be the case, remind them of the performance evaluation.

Sources for change will be quite numerous: your employees to start with but also your customers, your competition, your headquarters, and your imagination. You will need to employ quite an amount of change in order to achieve the ever increasing sales figure that will be required by the shareholders. Now, as always, prioritise and concentrate on a few practical steps not too difficult to implement rather than the big picture. The step by step approach is the best one, only because you have to deal with people and very few of them will be highly enthusiastic about modifying their habits. Therefore always consider how people will react and what resistance you will face. Here we come back to training and developing your branch into a learning organisation. Train people so they can improve and introduce ideas for change into your training programs. Involve as many people as possible as early as possible. Work into those training programs all the objections or resistance situations you might encounter.

Once more, time is of the essence. Think as an entrepreneur. Change is not free. You will be putting money on the table. What will be the return? Follow a good principle, which is really a saying now, "never change a winning proposition". Therefore only change if the added benefit to the bottom line is clear.

The picture below gives us a good example of how the life of bankers has changed. The author who published this picture in 1996 was so right; in fact the future model has already been the present model for a few years now.

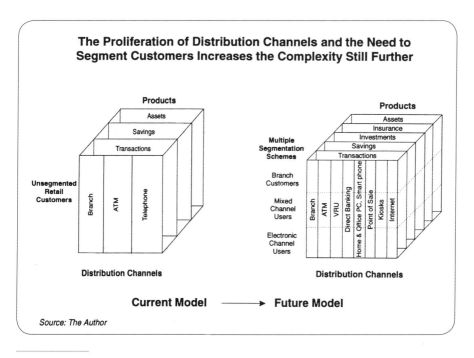

9) Distribution 2000 op.cit.

> Tip: Always be open about the need to change and about the successes or failure of the implementation. Make sure that all are aware of the results of changes, it is their future! Therefore report openly on the status of things and on the conclusions in relation to success or failure. Do not be afraid to change planned change, if need be. Only fools never change their mind. Do whatever is required to achieve your goals.

Think about time management again. Set yourself deadlines.

For all sorts of reasons, you may not be in a position to do something for a top performing employee. There is no room for training. The budget does not allow a salary increase. Whatever! Offer this employee the opportunity to rotate jobs. Job rotation not only provides the employee with a new challenge but likewise offer the possibility to learn something new, enhance future career moves and move into a learning curve.

People intuitively resist change but once their mind is set to it, they often achieve or surpass the expectations. Change should be part of corporate culture as should a permanent concern to find ways of improving whatever action is being taken. For this reason quality circles, whereby members brain storm on quality and performance improvement is a highly motivating exercise, especially when effects of change result in increased profits!

> A Tip: Quickly drop changes that do not work!

Change is such a significant component of business that this topic should definitely be part of the performance evaluation. It would be difficult to accept that a top performer would be resisting change, for instance. He should be a champion for change, when appropriate.

One change that you will undoubtedly need to introduce is the fact your branch is gradually going to move from a traditional bank outlet into a retail sales outlet! It means that you will need to look at your branch as a retailer! One example of this is how much are you selling per square meter? Another example: what channel is the cheapest? To what extent are your staff coping with this new role? ING, the large Dutch group has started a new experience on this front, which is a tremendous change versus what we are used to in branches, i.e. they organised a branch as a coffee outlet: one side of the place for coffees and the other side for financial products. You drop in for coffee at the coffee bar, check the stocks, bonds, whatever, and purchase a financial product. The experience is too recent to draw conclusions but you will certainly agree, this is a substantial change from the traditional dull branch!

Change means that today's approach is based on the following goals:
• Being closer to the customer
• Putting the accent on sales and advice
• Integrating all available branch and bank channels in your distribution

The fundamentals of good retailing are common to all across the board. Factors that play a critical role include[10]:
• Catchment's area (customer profiles)
• Share of catchment's area, called footfall in retailing (who comes in and when)
• How long customers stay, called dwell time in retailing
• Number of interactions with staff, called interception rate
• Average transaction value
• Waiting time
• Repeat purchase

"All of these are measurable and, with the exception of catchments, they can be directly influenced by design of any physical retail proposition. The best design always results from analysing in detail the needs of the end user, and tailoring the design strictly to those".[11] The question you might want to ask yourself is: "can my branch ever be a desirable place to be?" Would a customer feel as much at ease as in a chic boutique or in a comfortable meeting room, with glossy books and the smell of coffee? As people can shop around they will select a branch where they feel at home, a branch they enjoy visiting, and keep in mind, not necessarily with the cheapest products.

---

10) Peter Champion, First Partnership, London UK in "Branch Profitability", David Cavell, Lafferty Publications

11) Idem note 5

Change requires that the behaviour of yourself and your employees change! It is a matter of attitude and behaviour. One method of achieving this is to take a few branches that are operating in similar circumstances. Benchmark the best and have others compete to beat the benchmark. It is a useful exercise be it only to review why one branch is better than another branch and what could or should be done to reach or beat the benchmark.

Benchmarking is like ratios in financial analysis. They are only useful if used for the same type of branch, constantly adjusted and refined and compounded in the same way. Another advantage is that all branches will gradually move towards the same sort of level and that the organisation will have a harmonious branding in the market.

Providing clear communications to customers and employees

There are a number of ways that good communication can be achieved:

❏ Clear and positive leadership is required.

❏ The leadership should adopt a well-communicated and easy to understand mission.

❏ Subordinate goals to the mission are to be believable, relevant and demanding in terms of tasks that needs to be fulfilled in order to achieve it.

❏ Branch spirit programs to introduce participants to the business culture can be an important ingredient in establishing strategic plan goals.

❏ An initial approach to introducing strategic planning after commitment by top management is to gradually broaden the initial group to create a "central values" group, i.e. amongst others the key managers and branch managers.

Of paramount importance is the way the messages are communicated. Part of being a successful manager is communicating effectively. Communication is in fact ongoing. An account statement is a marketing tool. An internal marketing newsletter is by definition a communication tool. The same goes for your web site. However, what is perhaps overlooked is that the way your employees talk about you as a manager or about the bank in general, is also communication. It could be good, or poor, or negative advertising.

Good communication therefore requires that things are clear in your own mind. Make sure that this is the case before you communicate something and also make sure you follow up on how your message is being understood and or implemented. Therefore you need to be selective in communication and cut out everything which is not highly relevant.

Strangely enough communication means "listening first". Why? Because what you are stating – and you should only speak if it is really meaningful- should be regarded as trustworthy. Misunderstandings are often the result of poor listening. Keep an open mind on what you hear, you might gain something from it.

Communication is based on questions. Use the technique of varying your questions. It will help you in judging other people's performance better. You will recall the different type of questions, which are being used in selling techniques:

❑ Open questions (What would you ...if...?)

❑ Closed questions (Did you see the latest Dow quotation?)

❑ Fact-finding questions (How many times should the phone ring, before answering?)

❑ Follow-up questions (Did you rewrite this report?)

❑ Feedback questions (What is your impression on the last meeting?)

Employees are the organisation's most important assets. The interface of the branch with the other units of the organisation needs to be based on the above principles. Everyone is important and deserves a good, clear and professional communication. There should be no difference in the marketing support whether you are communicating externally or internally.

Good presentations will contribute not only to the acceptance of the message, the clearness of it all but likewise to the motivation of the employees.

Be aware that if you only get positive feedback, it might not be the truth! Make sure you get honest feedback. The best way to achieve this is to be honest yourself in what you say and do. We obviously assume that you act consequently, i.e. in line with what you are saying. Don't be afraid to discuss matters on the occasion of performance reviews, both with your own boss and with your subordinates.

The optimal branch structure

The structure should reflect the delegation of authority. Clear reporting lines are paramount, not just because they are required for efficiency reasons but because they will avoid conflicts and frustrations. Whilst people are in discussion time is going by and your income / cost relationship is suffering another blow.

A poor organisation contributes tremendously to under-performance. Therefore reporting lines should be short with as few intermediary levels as possible.

Increasing the use of distribution systems

In selecting a branch, a Canadian study showed that location, convenience, speed of service and the competence and friendliness of staff were key factors. Electronic financial services delivery changes lots of parameters but the main objectives are still there. Personal contact is now less frequent but its significance is therefore enhanced. Enhancing it even further, taking an active interest in the welfare of the customers, as far as this is possible, is a key element in building loyalty. Fortunately, people continue to play a key role despite all the automated delivery systems.

Based on various research studies, the following general statements can be made about:

Consumers' attitudes towards electronic distribution systems, retail branches and staff. These are :

– Consumers have become increasingly comfortable with electronic distribution systems
– Consumers expect and demand good service
– Consumers still expect and demand personal service for complex financial services

Utilisation of electronic distribution systems really depend on a variety of factors, which obviously include :

– age
– income
– previous usage of electronic distribution systems
– education
– place of residence

12) Idem (3)

One can generally observe that age is negatively correlated with use of electronic distribution systems and that income is positively correlated with usage of electronic distribution systems. Education, place and residence are weakly correlated with use of electronic distribution systems.

The multiplier effect should be kept in mind, i.e. usage of one or more electronic distribution systems, makes usage of additional systems more likely. The buyer's profile is evolving and should be monitored on a real-time basis.

Relative to this subject, let us examine the present thinking

The full service bank branch has been the conventional means of distributing banking and financial services. It has been effective for collecting and delivering cash and deposits, making loans and providing a range of services.

Using existing information about consumer needs and desires and anticipated shifts towards greater use of electronic distribution systems, it is possible to make some general projections of the way in which other channels will meet consumers' needs, the extent to which they are likely to be used, and their related cost structure.

Because of technology, banks will move from full control of all distribution channels to a much more extensive use of franchises. This does not entail blanket distribution to all customers, which would be far too expensive. It implies the ability to deliver to customers, identified as valuable, in the manner desired by those customers. **Identifying these preferences is one major challenge**.

The picture below underlines all the changes during the last 30 years. In fact since its publication in 1996 one has seen that virtual banks are not replacing the classical branches but that modern banking requires a different type of branch, more tuned to the day to day needs of customers than ever before with an increasing number of services provided automatically.[13]

---

13) Distribution 2000 op.cit.

77

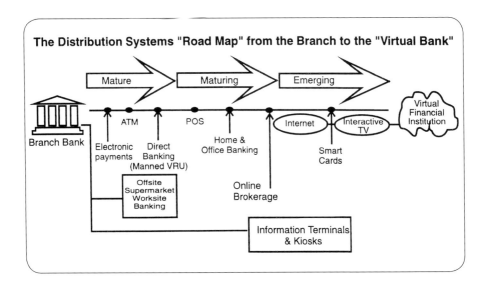

> *For virtually all transactions that are handled manually, both customers and financial institutions can benefit from the introduction of electronic systems. Consumers benefit from increased accuracy, speed and reduced transaction time. Institutions benefit from lower costs and increased accuracy.*

The challenge will be to make the appropriate decisions as to the present and future distribution environment, with an integrated segmentation, pricing and channel approach, consistent with the customer's experience.

Annual plans for the branch network should be prepared, measured and reviewed as though they were operating units with plans and budgets. It is important to ascertain how successful each branch is, relative to all others in the system. There are wide variations in the ways in which different banks accounting systems examine revenue and cost components.

Despite this, however, all branches should be ranked and reviewed against a common set of measures which can provide an equivalent assessment that "normalises" such factors as numbers of customers, types of customers,...Although branch staff and bank management may have general impressions of the branch and its market, the process of conducting a "formal review" of each branch is crucial to the understanding of the market, the customer base and competitors. In the process of analysing the competitors in a market, it is possible to develop a good understanding of their general business, as well as their distribution strategies.

Elements of analysis, besides the branch's balance sheet, are:

- ❑ local market physical facilities inventory
- ❑ service performed for other internal units
- ❑ transaction mix
- ❑ branch staff performance
- ❑ customer mix and customer prospect
- ❑ customer / product mix
- ❑ new customer acquisition
- ❑ competitors
- ❑ regulatory constraints
- ❑ best practice of best performing branches
- ❑ branch configurations

One good way to evaluate a branch is to examine its performance with "peer" group branches.

One dilemma facing future bank-branch planning is how to provide the sophisticated branch products needed to compete successfully. The answer is to introduce skilled sales personnel into the branch. The next dilemma is how to pay for the staff and tools required. There are only two options: reduce the need for conventional tellers and staff by shifting to self-service and remote transactions or absorb the increased costs. The latter is not possible in a highly competitive environment. Therefore, a further shift to self-transactions in branches will free transaction resources to pay for an increase in branch sales. This solution includes the possibility that some banks will see the introduction of branches without transaction personnel. This has been the strategy of some mutual funds providers. The next step will be to limit sharply branch personnel to essential customer interfaces and sales.

"Most existing branch offices operate on a supermarket product-pull model, in which people come into the store to buy specific products. The intention is for branches to become product-push retailers, serving as the place in which location-dependent activities that require personal service for target segments are conducted. Location-dependent activities include sales of more complex, higher added value products that are typically sold rather than bought. The branch should also provide a place in which customers can resolve problems that require face-to-face contact. Simple as this statement may appear, it includes a series of complex changes that need to occur.[14]"

In the meantime, it should be ensured that transactions still carried out at branch level are handled most efficiently, by speeding up teller transactions and encouraging customers to migrate to ATMs, i.e. electronic assisted transactions rather than operator assisted transactions. This implies quite a few changes for the branch staff as well as for the customers. To name just two, salespeople should be accessible at the hours when customers are most likely to want to meet them, including in the evenings and at week-ends; and salespeople need access to all of the modern electronic tools used by their most sophisticated customers. In view of this sales environment staff will require to be highly qualified.

The relationship managers require additional training beyond that offered to traditional branch staff. As well as standard product knowledge, relationship managers must have a good understanding of more sophisticated products and also need to be able to analyse a customer's financial needs. Training in financial planning, software, time management and contact management software can help managers and relationship managers to perform well.

One of the by-products of changing customers' transactions from manual to electronic is a sense of loss of control by the customer. This is particularly acute when problems or errors occur, as customers have often lost the personal relationship or face-to-face contact that previously existed. Customers often deliberately try to establish such personal contact with an individual in the branch, even if they do not

---

14) J. Svigals, Bank Branching 2010, Lafferty 1996

have a specific problem, so that they know and are known by a person who can help resolve a problem that might occur in the future.

This type of behaviour means that, as more activity shifts to electronic distribution systems, a conscious effort must be made to ensure high service quality and quick, efficient, courteous problem and error resolution. Customers expect errors and problems to occur; their perception of an institution is based on how well and how quickly problems can be solved. Research has shown that customer satisfaction levels are often higher after a problem has occurred, provided that the problem has been resolved quickly, efficiently and courteously.

The achievements of the past two decades have been significant and make the goals for the next decade of bank branching even more challenging.

"The bank branch will continue to be the crucial link in bank success. Branch Banking in 2010 will be as different as it was in 1970, 1980, and 1990. Think back and compare the differences. The changes are accelerating and the role of the banker is to stay ahead of the change process. To be forewarned is to be forearmed. The task is to recognise change for what it is - the demand for defining convenience and business content in a new time frame."

In any event the branch will increasingly focus on its most obvious role, i.e. selling

Branch design

The layout

"In a nutshell, people control sales, while design and layout control how the customer transacts with the institution"[18].

The physical layout of the branch needs to match the needs of your customer base. Its sales strategy should be reflected in the design of the delivery channels. Today, an increasing number of branches look like shops, a reflection of banking moving towards financial services, or retailing moving to retail shops.

Thinking as an "entrepreneur shopkeeper" is quite a step for branch managers. It means for instance that customers and shoppers, i.e. non customers are welcome. It means that if you manage a large enough branch, for instance, a children's play area is built into the design. The colour scheme should be in line with the company's image and branding. Of course, like any shop, you would have to promote quality products with well known brands!

The whole issue of layout is much more than just a matter of colours and attractive leaflets; it is an issue of branch effectiveness.

The design of a branch must be a combination of service based and of sales based space allocation. Retailing is about perception and influencing perception. The layout will contribute to this.

We should not forget that "banks" evoke many negative perceptions with the public. The way to change this is to give the consumers a different feel or touch or smell. Because products are not tangible, the experience of being in a branch should at least be tangible and a good and pleasant experience.

We underline the issue of the layout. A retail study showed on video that most foot traffic speeds up when passing bank premises. Hardly anybody looks at, let alone reads, the posters in bank windows! Nobody

---

18) Margaret Kane, Kane and Associates, Sacramento, US, in Branch profitability, Lafferty publications

walks into a bank unless they have a good reason for going inside. Nobody browses, strolls, in a bank branch. Customers find that bank premises are often uncomfortable, intimidating and want to leave as quickly as possible. It is just the opposite of "retailing" where the idea is that shoppers stay a while, see what is on offer and purchase. Design can change the unappealing image of banking, making it attractive. As an example look at the success of the cyber coffee shops! Think about cross selling. Most customers hardly ever purchase more than one or two products from the same bank. You might change this by giving your customer a welcoming and relaxing environment which encourages them to linger. Most people have financial needs but never really sit down and think about it. A pleasant branch might be the perfect place to do just that.

A success in this field is Abbey National in the UK, which really applied the tips of the most successful retailers:

- Open welcoming frontage

- Minimum obstruction to the entrance

- Bold, illuminated fascia and dynamic messages

- Bright and warm lighting

Having achieved the hardest part, make them stay! The environment must be inviting with a certain ambience and comfort. Graphics and signage can help in making the "potential customer" at home or provide him with an excuse for being there. Those looking for basic, efficient service need a fast track process. The most appealing thing the retailer has to show is his staff, especially now that products are intangible, i.e. services. A dear friend was working in the City of London and told us that the branch where she maintained her account had a real coal fire. She thought it was wonderful on a cold winter's day. "You did not want to go out again!" She felt it was also good to talk to staff who are not behind bars!

Waiting time if advice is required is almost unavoidable. Make sure the customer uses that time in an optimal way by looking at a video or by surfing on your web site! Teller queues should not be part of the image you strive to promote. Make sure as few people as possible use tellers. If there is a need to wait give them a number and have them waiting in comfortable, friendly surroundings. It will also reduce their frustration in having to wait. They might learn something in the meantime which could lead you to another sale. A study of a possible layout is provided below. We start looking at branches as retailers do at their shops[19].

> "Most people find their finances a drag. So, if they can go to a brand that they respect and trust, which treats them like an individual, which is expert, efficient, and innovative, offers reasonable value, they will seldom go elsewhere. They will be brand oriented and be prepared to pay more for certain products rather than less"[20].

The picture below indicates the relationship between lay-out and the speed of services delivered. This is a retailer's approach. Question: do all branches need to have the same layout? Experience has shown this is not the case[21].

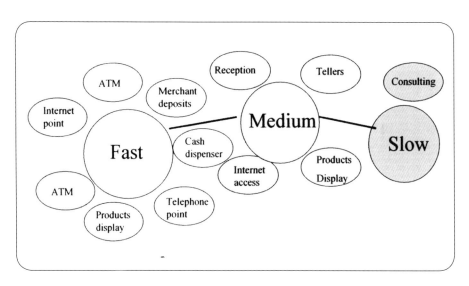

19) Bank Branching 2010, op. cit.

20) Peter Champion, First Partnership, London, UK, in Branch profitability, David Cavell, Lafferty Publications.

21) J. Svigals: " Bank Branching 2010", Lafferty Publications.

Using local marketing tools efficiently and effectively

Using the telephone

Here follow a few tips from various courses on "phoning", which everyone, not just telephone operators, should master:

Keep a clock on your desk to make you aware of how fast time goes and how expensive your call will be; think and teach your employees to think as "entrepreneurs", which means "I" not the branch (even if it is a branch expense) am spending so much, what will I get out of it? Is it worth the investment? Supposing you talk for quarter of an hour without a tangible aim, what is the price of that call? The answer is: obviously the invoiced amount of the telephone company but also your cost to the organisation. In the EU for an average branch manager that would amount to about 13.50 Euro per quarter of an hour + overhead expenses + head quarter's expense allocation, say roughly the double of that amount, i.e. 27 Euro, totalling about 40 Euro! Even if those figures prove inflated, you will see that in any event this is an investment well above the pure price tag of the telephone conversation.

Prepare your call. Know what you want to achieve, makes notes to the file and follow up. If you promise something, ensure you do it and follow-up. Make sure the message is well received, clearly analysed and understood. Misunderstandings will in all likelihood double your cost!

Advertising

At branch level you will probably seldom have to initiate and print your own brochures. In all likelihood, they will be provided by headquarters. However, you are a user to the same extent as the customers and prospects, for whom these brochures are intended. So **be constructively critical** in order to help the marketing people to produce what matches your needs as effectively as possible.

What type of improvements could you and your staff consider? Does the brochure clearly describe the product and does the product match the needs of the customers? Are the brochures creative enough or are they dull? Are they attractive? What are the customer's comments? You are an essential source of information for the marketing department. Do not forget: marketing is not the responsibility of the marketing department; it is the responsibility of every single employee. Your feedback is essential. Who knows the customer better than you do? You have two types of customers, internal and external customers. Both should be accorded the same attention, be treated on the same ground. Are your communications to your staff as attractive as your brochures are to your customers?

The relationship between the branch and the central marketing department

There could very well be some conflict of interest between the central marketing department and the branch as certain commercial actions may be planned centrally and not necessarily in line with your specific plan or serving area. Also you might want to put the accent on some reachable objectives in the short run whereas the bank might be more interested for the time being in for instance branding-

Dialogue is the response. It works both ways. It is the duty of the marketing department to explain to the field what they plan and why. It is the duty of the field to explain what is expected by customers and prospects.

In any event there should never be a situation of "us and them" or "the field and the headquarters"! As branch manager it is undoubtedly one of your responsibilities to explain your situation and it is the central departments' duty to listen to what you have to say. It is your boss's duty to ascertain that this is happening and if this is not the case to intervene in the name of his managers.

Planning

A business plan is a document where aims and objectives are clearly set out! In respect of the format, you may want to take a look at the part of this book relative to the sales process. Always clearly outline the goals, the problems likely to be encountered in reaching the goals, the information required to ensure that people will understand the issues and the likely outcome. You must show that you have a good grasp of financial issues; that you have considered most factors which might affect your plan and obviously what the consequences will be to your profit and loss account in the best and worst cases.

Planning also involves some strategy vis-à-vis your supervisors. Do not forget that during the year following your plan it would be more pleasant to explain why you are above plan rather than why you are below plan! Therefore plan on the conservative side, do not be over optimistic and make sure you have a defence in the event of misfortune.

---

22) Hyrum Smith, "Natural laws of successful time and life management", Time Warner.

Be honest when describing the current situation. Planning rests on developing an intuition for months to come. It will be affected by so many elements that predicting beyond a year or two is hazardous. Now, despite this, there is a need for a long term strategy and a short term plan. Our view is that the branch's concern is mainly short term with the additional dimension that it needs to be integrated into the organisation's long term plan.

In any event, the greatest added value of a plan is the questions you will have been asking yourself. For an organisation which has never planned, it takes a few years to get used to planning and to make sure planning becomes part of the branch's culture. When you have reached that stage, you will wonder how you ever lived without a plan and how you could ever have measured performance improvement.

Some questions you should be asking yourself are:

- What exactly is the key goal of the business?
- How good is the marketing concept?
- How difficult will it be to market my products?
- What are my goals?
- Do I have the required skills and abilities?
- What will be my cash needs?
- Am I willing to take time to plan my success?

Your business plan helps you to be sure your business is carefully planned and makes sense, both from a financial and operative perspective. The business plan is your game plan. It also acts as a standard against which to compare your actual results with your anticipated results. Regularly comparing your plans with actual results will allow you to identify problems quickly, often before they become unmanageable. Each year, update your plan using the informal business plan as a guide. That way you will always stay on track and your business will do well!

Another advantage is that your plan will help you explain your ideas to your superiors, colleagues and staff.

Targets are vital to the whole branch. Therefore everyone should be involved, whatever the position held. Everyone should also feel that if the branch achieves its goals, they will, as individuals, be able to reach their professional as well as their private goals.

Plan to maximise your earnings and minimise your expenses, along the same lines as entrepreneurs. This really comes down to shifting high cost – low income customers to automated distribution channels, or loosing them and improving the return from low cost –high income customers. We are back to marketing. In order to achieve this you need to know your customers. You need to have segmented them and profiled them, You need to train your staff and in some ways train your customers so that they select the right product and the right distribution channel. In other words, you need to have done your home work as a marketing adept entrepreneur!

Every organisation will have its own system but that does not necessarily mean that all branches should plan exactly the same way. Indeed branches may have a very different customer base and a very different profile and distribution pattern. Some will therefore have to concentrate more on service; hence their cost /return ratio may be lower than other branches. Others will be in a position to concentrate more on automated services. One should take these marketing considerations into account when analysing the performance of branches of the same bank. They are all branches but not necessarily the same sort of branch.

If the branch and the organisation is set up to provide for substantial information (through a MIS, management information system) you might consider a profit model for your customers, which should include:
• Account revenue,
• Transaction and maintenance cost at customer level.
• Retail segmentation information (age, education, wealth, life stage)
• You should take into account the traditional data as to account balances, account turnover, overdrafts, etc. Altogether that would give you a good base from which to start your planning.

An IBM UK[23] study showed that there is a correlation between business performance and the customer management score, hence the branch management. The strongest correlation occurred when the following were present:
• Strong leadership
• Management competence
• People with clear objectives (remember MBO)
• Reliable performance measurement
• Excellent customer management activities (enquiries, new products explanation, pro-activity, …)

23) Branch Profitability, David Cavell, Lafferty Publications

Finally recall that a goal should be a "SMART" thing to achieve. We mean a goal should be

♦ Specific

♦ Measurable

♦ Acceptable to both parties

♦ Realistic

♦ Timed

Job descriptions

Goal setting starts with job description because it provides an objective basis for evaluating and improving performance. It enhances the team spirit. It provides for a fair basis of control and audit and above all it helps in determining the needs of the branch. This assumes that the marketing analysis has been accomplished with the study of relevant threats and opportunities.

Job descriptions establish a clear link to the organisational goals; determine what needs to be accomplished; define where the responsibilities lie and the accountabilities as well as the expectations of every single position within the branch. Job descriptions are highly valuable in determining if a job is really necessary or if it can be merged with another job, or can be enhanced or eliminated.

To produce or evaluate a job description always proceed with questions. A good example would be the job description of a person responsible for sales. We would ask ourselves the following questions:

What are the various tasks required from that salesperson?

- Sales, of course
- Account administration
- Credit administration
- Customer service
- Personal development

What would we expect from sales?

- Identify needs of existing and potential customers
- Cross sell
- Upgrade existing relationships
- Handle requests from existing and potential customers
- Be familiar with product information and development
- Report to the marketing and other department relevant data
- Represent the bank whenever there could be a direct or an indirect sales opportunity

91

You can ask more questions but do not forget that the purpose of it all is performance enhancement. So we need to measure what is really going to make a difference. We need to ask the questions which are really relevant to that goal.

Further questions, for instance, on personal development!

How does a person participate in internal training programs?

How willing is a person to participate in external, outside working hours or self learning programs?

How motivated is a person in knowing the latest on product development, on policies?

The result of this effort is like a "swot" (strength, weakness, opportunities and threats) analysis. It gives a base on which to start your measurement. We are close to add numbers and deadlines. In the meantime, the regional offices or divisions are making comparisons and are in a position to establish benchmarks.

You can go into the fine detail but only measure what enables change for the sake of improvement!

This exercise at branch level will enable the organisation to establish benchmarks and analyse gaps between those benchmarks and the facts. It will enable senior management to take into account specific factors. Much more than that it will force the employees to marry their perception of things with the bank's perception of what is expected from them. It will be a sound basis for performance evaluation and allow for the best motivator, i.e. management per objectives.

Determining goals

Goal setting is the result of :
- A decision on what to measure
- A decision on how to measure
- Having set up a reliable MIS (management information system)

Measures should be:
- Qualitative
- Quantitative

Let us stay with sales (this is the key thing anyway)
- Qualitative measures would result from the following issues
- Development of prospects
- Allocation of time
- Specific sales calls on segmented customers/prospects
- Promptness and completeness of sales call reports
- Accuracy and completeness of customer records
- Development of product, market and competitor knowledge

Quantitative measures would result from the following information
- Total sales volume
- Sales volume by type of product
- Number of account relationships
- Sales volume per sale
- Number of sales calls
- Sales expenses as percent of sales volume

Once this is clearly defined for all, you may get to performance goals, i.e. you know where you are and can determine where you want to be at the end of the period.

Your goals will only be effective if:
- They are specific with time constraints
- Challenging
- Accepted
- Individual
- Used
- Supported by yourself as branch manager
- Transparent
- Controllable by all involved

You are familiar now with the ABC of goal setting; the next thing is doing it, which remains the best way to learn!

From individual goals you will determine the goals of the team and finally with the inclusion of your own goals the goals of the branch. Make sure those goals are discussed and reviewed on an on-going basis and are part of the day to day life of the branch.

SUMMARY STEP BY STEP GOAL SETTING

1st   *Determine the goals by means of a swot and questions*

2nd   *Determine qualitative and quantitative goals*

3rd   *Plan the implementation in a time frame*

4th   *Control in a time frame*

5th   *Establish accountability*

6th   *Determine alternative actions*

7th   *Communication and information to all involved*

Observation and feedback

There will be a gap between your plan and reality. Therefore, ongoing monitoring is a must. This will, as usual, be based on questions! Maybe the goals were not right in the first place? Why? Have you been overoptimistic? Maybe you overestimated your catchment area? Whatever, ask questions till you find the right answer. Assuming your goals were impeccably set, what are the reasons for the gap: Maybe the environment, the economic cycle, the product line, the morale? Find out and fix it. It is possible.

In order to do this efficiently you need information in the form of activity reports and records. They will provide you with the required support for the analysis of the gap. In this respect, it makes no difference whether your gap is positive or negative. Both situations require an analysis and an evaluation.

Fixing the gap between actual performance and planned performance is management

Performance measurement

The goal of performance measurement should not be just a quantitative exercise, often referred to as a "number crunching" exercise but it should aim at transforming performance by measuring and managing the drivers of business success.

Basically we encounter two key questions: (1) Can measurement drive internal change, improve performance and the delivery of capabilities whilst allowing for excellence? (2) How might it positively influence or change behaviour?

There is no point measuring quality or making improvements if they do not impact on business performance and profitability, if they do not contribute to excellence and/or branding.

> *Measures should be developed for the things we should be doing, not just what one is doing.*

The usual shortcomings are over- or under-measurement or focusing on the wrong type of issues, which are not aligned with business strategy, performance and profitability nor have a link with competitive issues.

"One of the weaknesses of the banking industry is that our traditional performance measures have always been biased towards external financial reporting. They have not measured broader value in terms of quality, service and speed. Financial measures have not led us to innovate or learn, or motivate longer-term behaviours and strategies.[24]"

> *All forms of measurement should lead to excellence & cover the following nine (9) values which constitute an excellent checklist indeed.*

24) Roger Bosworth, director NatWest UK in "Growing Brand Loyalty" by Richard H Evans, Lafferty Publications, April 1997.

Leadership

How the behaviour and actions of the branch manager inspire, support, and promote a culture of total quality management. Staff will only be able to perform outstandingly, when there is a clear understanding of the performance you expect from them and how they can accomplish it.

Leadership is concerned with communicating desired performance objectives and providing your staff with the help needed to accomplish those objectives. Bear in mind that your staff can accomplish much more as a team than when they work separately. Leadership is concerned with reconciling the interest and objectives of the branch so that each can contribute productively to the performance of the whole bank.

What does leadership imply for you as a branch manager and how can the performance be assessed?

Here are some key areas of performance measurement:
– Be people oriented
– Develop people
– Persuade rather than command
– Communicate with clarity
– Encourage participation and initiative
– Have realistic performance expectations
– Set high standards of personal performance

Of course, every point could be developed. Let us look again at the branch manager relative to the first point for a change. Be people oriented means:
– Be concerned with understanding of the individual needs of your staff and helping them in satisfying those needs
– Recognise individual differences and capabilities in people, and adjust the supervision accordingly
– Avoid judging people
– Be really interested in the progress of your staff
– Be ready to help your staff in solving problems

In some organisations branch managers are evaluated by their staff in the same way as the staff is evaluated by management. If you are being evaluated it will be quick and clear! Rest assured people will not miss your weak points. Such is life. If you are not "formally" evaluated, people will do it anyway and you will have to rely on "hear-say", a very bad way of getting to know things.

Other points of the analysis

– **Organisation**: How the organisation formulates, deploys, reviews, and turns policy and strategy into plans and actions at various levels of the organisation and ultimately at branch level

– **People management**

  How the organisation realises the full potential of its people.

– **Resources**

  How the organisation manages resources effectively and efficiently

– **Processes**

  How the organisation identifies, manages, reviews and improves its processes

– **Customer satisfaction**

  What the organisation is achieving in relation to the satisfaction of its external customers

– **Employee satisfaction**

  What the organisation is achieving in relation to the satisfaction of its staff

– **Impact on society**

  What the organisation is achieving in satisfying the needs and the expectations of the local & national community

– **Business results**

  What the organisation is achieving in relation to its planned business objectives and in satisfying the needs and expectations of everyone with a financial interest or other stake in the organisation

An example for a measurement methodology is the system designed by the European Foundation for Quality Management. One will notice that 50 % of the points are represented by the "business enablers" and the other 50% by results but measured only up to 15 % in what is generally referred to as "profits"!

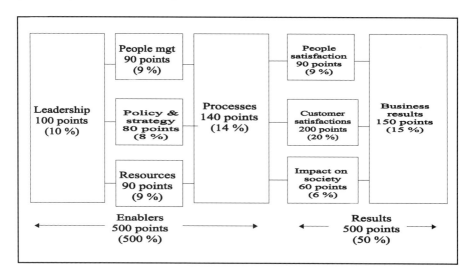

People issues appear to be "make or break factors" in success. Therefore deliberate, targeted and ongoing communication strategies are crucial, along with education and reinforcing a central question: *How does individual effort relate and contribute to business strategy?*

You will realise that the search for excellence and outstanding performance focuses on:
→ business volume
→ value of client assets
→ retention
→ satisfaction survey ratings
→ service standards
→ audience perception

→ recognition of client needs
→ innovation
→ project process
→ internal customer relations
→ credit quality

25) Business Intelligence, Strategic performance measurement, Chris Ashton, 1997
    This scheme is a registered trade mark and is only mentioned here as an indicative example of a way of thinking about an overall performance of an entity, be it a branch or a much larger organisation.

Let us take one item of this list, say, employee measurement as a point in case:

First step: **value** people, measurement through regular surveys & feedback

Second step: **evaluate** effectiveness of people as per their individual skills & training

Third step: individual & **team** performance measurement in line with expected results

These three steps require the measurement of the following values in relation to the others:
– mutual respect
– integrity
– trusting people and earning their trust
– being open and approachable
– treating everyone fairly
– working together
– fostering teamwork
– encouraging initiative and innovation
– taking pride in work
– determination in achieving goals
– clear direction
– encouragement and recognition
– visible support and training

Measuring should lead to a culture change. Companies should focus on: a performance-oriented culture through management based on coaching instead of command; rewarding team-work instead of individual performance, learning and development being aligned to individual and business needs.

We should move towards a consultant-type of relationship with key staff, as a first step. We should consider that measurement, in principle, must drive performance improvement, thus acting as a means to an end.

Besides, performance evaluation will be an incredibly useful feedback as well a management instrument. It will also be a very powerful motivational instrument. In the short run, setting it up will take a lot of time but in the long run it will be an indispensable tool of management.

Scorecard

Based on the evaluation of various criteria, you could set up a scorecard for your branch. The key components of a scorecard should have the following items:

- Production
- Implementation of goals
- Customer satisfaction
- Control
- Staff performance
- Procedural issues

The scorecard is in fact the summary of all the individual performance appraisals. The goal is to improve on the present scoring! It is also for the organisation an incredibly efficient tool to measure performance overall and on a comparative basis between the various branches. The scorecard therefore becomes the benchmark and decreases the purely subjective part inherent to any evaluation. A scorecard looks like an "excel table", where you would list the relevant components of your branch and receive a rating per component. The rating would be the result of your assessment of your team, of their assessment of the situation in the branch, of audit and control, of the regional head, etc.

It is up to the organisation which points are to be incorporated in the scorecard and which norms are applicable per subject: for instance, personnel management. The measured items would be

- Personnel satisfaction
- Training on the job and outside
- Team spirit
- Communication
- Flexibility

Needless to say, if the individual reports are weak so will be the overall situation. This state of affairs can only improve from the bottom up! Let us take training.

You would score above average if:
- You actively share your knowledge
- You actively participate in the goal setting of your employees
- You are innovative and demanding

You would score below average if:
- You do not recognise talent and develop opportunities
- You do not reach your own objectives
- You are not able or capable of listening

Revenues

> *We are in business to make money. As manager, making money is your primary concern. The issue is not just the profit and loss account of your branch but also your career and your credibility as a branch manager.*

There are only two routes to success: either increase your income or decrease your expenses. As the former is, generally speaking, more difficult and time consuming, examine your expenses the way you look at marketing issues, i.e. with questions! Do you really need to take a certain action? What about omitting it? What would be the consequence? What would be the impact on the consumers, on the employees and on your profit and loss account (P&L)?

Questions! Question everything you do and ask if it could be done in a cheaper, faster or more efficient way. You should, even if your bank is organised differently, think as a chief executive, responsible for the daily balance sheet and the profit and loss account. A key measure here of your success is the cost / income ratio of the branch.

The main reason for failure at branch level is undoubtedly a lack of management focus on what makes a truly successful branch, i.e. people and process. Reduce personnel to the minimum but as a professional branch manager actively manage the personnel you have. Think in this instance as a true entrepreneur, i.e. in net present value terms.

Let us consider an example

Take a direct mailing to 1.000 selected customers. By the way, this means that you know your customers and that you have segmented them according to specific criteria. How much are you putting on the table? Such an example in Belgium would cost about 2.500 Euro. It may seem a lot but you have to take all costs into account, i.e. stamps, printing, envelopes, brochure printing cost, etc.) Assuming senior management wants a return of say 10%, it would mean that you must generate 250 Euro on that investment "on an annual basis". Experience has shown that you are likely to obtain a 5% response ratio. This means that 50 people will react to your proposal. Let us assume you are not just an outstanding branch manager but also a good salesman. You have systematically called all the persons who received your mail. You convinced 20% of the respondents to purchase the product you are proposing. This means that you will have 10 new customers from whom you will have to make 250 Euro or 25 Euro per customer, just to cover that specific marketing action. You will have noticed that we did not mention the other essential costs such as your salary over the period, the overheads of the branch, telephone expenses, nor the headquarters expenses and marketing development expenses. If you take all those expenses into account you might well triple that amount. Let us say you thus need 75 Euro per customer for that product. Can you achieve it? Let us say that the very product you were presenting was a credit card. Your fee on such a card would be about 20 Euro. So you need to be very confident that the customer is going to use his card and be in debit for the additional 55 Euro, which means an almost permanent outstanding debit balance, of about 400 Euro!

You can apply this type of analysis to many situations. Do not get too weighed down by detailed figures. If you have your costs well in hand your approximation will be a good and often sufficient guide to make managerial decisions. In real estate the saying goes that the best budgets are done on the back of an envelope! This means that a sound, with feet on the ground analysis, is often sufficient and will not be materially different from sophisticated computer planning.

Management Background

The net present value concept

Human capital is composed of knowledge, ability, talent, expertise, management skill, brilliance or insight. **Strangely enough, we often make the statement in the EU that we have discouraged the entrepreneurs because of administrative burdens, high social security contributions and high taxation. You might apply that statement to many financial institutions as well, because of burdensome procedures, rules and the legal framework.** *The future of Europe will depend upon a correction in this field. It is essential that entrepreneurs are encouraged to start their own businesses and find financing in order to do so. This differentiates Europe from the USA, where 35 percent of students leaving Harvard Business School start their own companies versus less than 5 percent of the university students in Europe. The entrepreneur is also someone who will continuously strive to balance flexibility and cost cutting in order to discover the optimal structure of the branch, pushing for productivity, which is "the" competitive asset of an organisation. However, the entrepreneurs know that their efforts are only worth it if they recover their initial investment and a return. As our regions have known inflation for hundreds of years, they also know that the purchasing power of the money they will generate in the future is decreasing over time.*

The present value concept (PV)

Let us assume you are an entrepreneur and you invest 100 monetary units in a project. For the sake of this example let us assume that this equates to purchasing a long-term bond. You are only going to do this if you recover your 100 units plus something more called a profit or a risk premium or interest.

Let us assume that you get 5 per annum out of this investment over a period of 10 years. That would mean in the 10 years you receive 10 times 5 plus at the end of that period, you get the initial investment back, i.e.100. But is the last payment of 5 worth as much as the first 5 or the second payment of 5? If our entrepreneur compares a payment of 5 of year 1 with a payment of say year 6, he is comparing apples and pears. Each of the 5s has a different purchasing power. What will be the purchasing power of the 5 in the future and what will be the purchasing power of 100 he receives back in ten years from now? The difference in purchasing power is due to inflation, which gradually erodes it. So an entrepreneur has to think in present value terms.

In an inflationary environment the present value of 5 one year from now is less than 5. In that type of environment a monetary unit of today is worth more than a unit of tomorrow. A unit of today can be invested today and start earning interest.. The level of interest will be related to the level of inflation. This is the first basic principle of Finance.

Thus, the present value of a delayed payoff may be found by multiplying the payoff by a discount factor. If C1 denotes the expected payoff at a period 1 (one year from now) then the present value is:

Present Value (PV) = discount factor x C1

*his discount factor is the value of a monetary unit received in the future. It is expressed as the **reciprocal of 1 + r (interest rate).***

Discount factor = $\dfrac{1}{1+r}$

"r" is the rate of return the entrepreneur is expecting from his investment or alternatively, is the rate of return he demands for accepting delayed payment.

The net present value concept (NPV)

Let us assume that the entrepreneur is tempted to invest in a project, which will generate in a year's time 400.000. Let us assume that the inflation rate is 7 % and that his goal is to keep up with inflation. The present value of that income, which will be paid one year from now is:

$$PV = \text{discount factor} \times C1 = \frac{C_1}{1+r} \quad \frac{400.000}{1+0.07} = 373.832$$

The 400.000 he will receive in one year is worth in today's terms: 373.832. Or in other words, by investing today 373.832 he will get 400.000 a year from now. But he will have made no profit. If he wishes to make a profit on top of keeping up with inflation he will have to think in net present value terms. Let us assume that by investing 350.000 he gets 400.000 in one year. Is it worth it? Yes, in net present value terms this is a good investment. His net cash out is 350.000 and his income is 373.000 in today's terms. The NPV is:

NPV = PV – required investment = 373.832 - 350.000 = 23.832

As far as expenses are concerned, always, always think as an entrepreneur. "I put so much on the table: what do I get out of it, when and what does this equate to in present value terms?"

The value of time

> *The second key issue for a branch manager is thinking about "time" as an expense or an investment. What is the cost of one hour of your time as a manager and what is the return?*

In the EU one hour of a manager's time quickly amounts to about 60 Euro on the assumption that the manager works 200 days per annum, and 6 hours "effectively" during the day. We are at about one Euro per minute. It would be fun (?) to make that calculation for all the staff of the branch and put it on a clock in the office!

This was once done in New York, at Times' Square where a clock showed the US indebtedness. People were rather shocked to see that the country's indebtedness was increasing at about USD 40.000 per minute! But the public was made aware that the country was living well above its means. The proof is that they put the clock away, so that they were no longer reminded of the fact.

Another example of entrepreneurial thinking relative to "time" is the cost of a meeting. Have you ever calculated the cost of a meeting? Let us give you a rule of thumb. Say there are five people at the meeting. Take their annual cost (i.e. gross salary + overhead expenses). Divide that amount by, say 200 (the number of working days over which those expenses can be spread). Divide that amount by 6 (the number of hours where people have "effectively" worked- in certain companies 6 is even generous but not generous for branch managers, who usually work much more than that!) That number would provide you with the cost of one hour meeting, which –thinking as an entrepreneur- needs to be offset by a matching income, at least.

Cost consciousness

The entrepreneur is obsessed by cost. The reason is that bills pour in: telephone, car maintenance, hardware and software, you name it. They pile up quickly and impressively. On the other side of the coin you have customers who tell you that "yes, the product seems interesting, I am going to think about it!" Strange how their time span seems to be different than yours! They seldom seem in a hurry, whilst your creditors are! Lack of income keeps entrepreneurs awake in the middle of the night!

The larger the corporation the fewer employees are really concerned about cost; as if cost was the concern of management and not of their own. As an entrepreneur if you have to call, say internationally, you are going to think about it first, keep it as short as possible and note that you have once more put so much on the table. You wonder to what extent this call is going to pay-off and above all when this call is going to pay off! In a large corporation, people just call because they feel they have to call and even take some time to chat about the weather or about the latest promotions or rumours in the organisation. After a few minutes, you will hear: "by the way I called you to see if you received that last report on the meeting of etc. None of the actors here would put the phone down and think about the cost involved and the fact that they could have saved the corporation some money by being brief and to the point.

> *Strangely enough people seem to think, once they have been hired, that money is not really their concern but the concern of senior management!*

For this reason they burden the system and are faced with cyclical redundancies. Most companies go down because of excessive cost, either operational or financial, not to speak about lack of organisation and administrative discipline!

Cost consciousness is a matter of attitude. It is the opposite of the attitude one would commonly find in administrations, where work seems to be created for the sake of it and for the careers of the responsible officers within the administration. Make sure you are not the only one in your branch to be obsessed with cost; everybody should be as everyone contributes to the goals of the branch and shares the same responsibility!

Preparing a business plan

The major task of a branch manager is to increase, even substantially, the revenues of the branch. This undoubtedly requires the knowledge of the main characteristics of his serving area. Furthermore, he needs a good grasp of the competence of his staff as they will greatly influence not only the achievement of demanding goals but also of the type of products the branch will be in a position to sell best.

The basic principles of a business plan

1. Determine the revenues generated by the existing portfolio

2. Compare the achieved data with the figures to be attained during the next period

3. The difference will be the additional revenue to be generated either by increasing sales of by decreasing cost

4. The difference will mean production targets per product

5. Spreading of those product related goals amongst the members of the team

The plan will be reviewed on a monthly basis. It will be subject to discussion in line with market and product realities. Amendments could be agreed upon with senior management on solid grounds.

On the basis of the figures on the opposite page we propose that you review the following practical case based on the retail banking approach.

These figures reflect revenues generated on a product basis for a retail branch in 2004.

The amount of revenues, in 2004, is 1.794.527 €. The year before, 2003, the amount of revenues was 2.016.067 €. The revenues of 2004 are thus only 89 % of the revenues of the year 2003.

---

26) Certain retailers only focus at branch level on revenues. Cost is a central issue at corporate level. Others allow local managers to optimize cost at branch level.

Calculation date: Year to Date 2004-12-31

	Branch	This Year 1,794,527	Last Year 2,016,067	
	Result in %	89,01% Objective in %	100% Variance	89,01% — Euro '000

Category	This Year	%	Item	This Year	Obj%	Item	Last Year	Var%	Item	Euro '000	%
Liabilities **46,16%**	828,346	-10%									
CA cr	24,472	+51%	PCA Cr	248,441	-1%	PCBA Cr	82,704	-4%	CA Fx Cr	67,151	-1%
MMA	61,252	-24%	MMA Fx	57,837	-32%	SAV	240,701	-24%	CD	44,864	
			BB	919	-32%	Other	0	-100%			
Assets **34,93%**	626,881	-1%									
CA Dt	5,231	-12%	PCA Dt	12,216	-8%	PCBA Dt	2,448	-92%	CAFX Dt	1,212	-55%
REV	73,752	-4%	Asrd REV	11,669	+5%	STL	347,36	+5%	ML	12,334	+19%
			Visa	160,654	+6%	Com Loans	0				
Fee bus. **18,91%**	339,299	-29%									
Funds Sales	111,861	-62%	Funds Pft	172,613	+29%	Share	6,063	-66%	Life	41,578	+70%
			Insur. 23	7,183	+88%						

Your objective for 2005 has been based on the figures of 2004. You should reach 106% i.e. 1.794.527 x 106% = 1.902.198 €.

The document is divided in three parts: Liabilities, Assets and Fees.

Liabilities

This item comprises everything which is related to "deposits" in the branch, be it in EURO or foreign currency. The items CA Cr (current account credit), PCA Cr (current packaged account credit), PCBA Cr. (current business account credit) represent the revenues generated by deposits on current account in EURO. The item CA FX Cr (current account foreign exchange credit) represents the same products but in foreign currency.

The items MMA (money market account in Euro) MMA FX (money market account in foreign currency) represent the revenues generated by time deposits at "attractive rates for customers", respectively in EURO and in foreign currencies. The same concept is valid for the SAV (saving products), CD (certificate of deposits) or term deposits and BB (bearer bills) for treasury notes. The item "Others" only represents products which can not be placed into above mentioned categories. It is normally zero, which is the case here.

All the items in the liabilities are by essence components of the branch's portfolio. The revenues[27] are generated by the assets of your customers, which are your branch's liabilities. This is part of the heritage which you have gained from your predecessor.

The revenue of all the products is represented by the "spread", i.e. the difference between the rate offered to the customer and the cost of funds to the bank in the money or capital market. It is this spread which highlights the fact that money deposited in your branch on a current account is much more profitable than money deposited in a savings account or in a fixed time deposit. Indeed, for the same amount you would grant a customer 0.5% on the current account whereas you have to grant about 2.5% in the second case. The item which will generate

---

27) In another system this could be considered as cost of funding, i.e. a cost even at branch level and not a revenue. This approach is a "retail" approach were every product, be it at the asset side or at the liability side of the balance sheet is considered as a revenue generating item for the organisation.

the lowest revenue for the branch is the term deposit as the customer will receive the highest rate.

As a matter of fact, as branch manager you have no influence on the "spread". Its level is determined by the central treasury department of the bank is a function of market circumstances.

This system forces the branches to attract cheap funds as it enhances their revenues. The only way to increase these items is to gain new customers whilst simultaneously maintaining the existing ones. Assuming the spread remains constant, your revenues should gradually increase (1.000.000 € increase on your savings accounts would generate 20.000 € per annum).

Obviously it is not through the "Liabilities" that you will be able to increase the profitability of your branch in the short term. Therefore you will have to put the accent on the asset side of your business for marketing actions. However, the concern for a stable and growing funding base is the "bread and butter" of your activities as it assures the long term viability of your branch, not to mention yours as branch manager.

Please note how much your life will be dependant upon the interest rates. Indeed the results of the branch will be subject to upwards or downwards fluctuations of the interest rates, hence the upwards or downwards movements of the spread.

Assets

Assets are mainly constituted by all forms of credit extension. The items CA DT (current account debit), PCA DT packaged current account debit), PCBA DT (packaged current business account) and CA FX are the mirror items of those mentioned in the liabilities. Here you find the revenues generated by the interest paid by your customers in the framework of your credit extension.

The item REV (revolving credit) and Insurance on loans due refer to customers who enjoy a credit line without connection to the current account. O/L Ins. represents the commission that you receive on the premium related to insurance that customers have to take out when they borrow in order to cover death or long term illness and thus consequent incapacity to repay the outstanding loan. In that case the insurance company would take over the obligation and repay the outstanding loan in lieu of the borrower.

The item ML (mortgage loan) represents the revenue generated by the portfolio relative to mortgage loans. VISA represents the use by your customers of their credit card facility. STL (short term loans) combines revenues from short term credits and commissions relative to those credits (same concept that REV, cf. supra).

We assume the bank is presently not extending credits to small enterprises and corporations at branch level which explains why the item Com Loan is blocked at zero.

Here again, as for the liabilities the branch's results are subject to the movements of the "spread".

The only item you can really influence with your sales force is the increase in loans and related insurance commissions (those which cover your short term credits: STL) Commissions are quite attractive to the branch. Indeed in this specific case 66 % of the premium paid by the customer constitutes revenue to the branch. Therefore in this particular case it will be your focal point.

Fees

Here we have two types of activities. The item "Life" is linked to commission earned whilst selling life assurance policies, not related to a credit product. All the other items are commissions generated by the sale of investment products such as investment funds, individual shares and bonds or investments via insurance policies and management fees on portfolios.

Here, the level of income depends on the percentage of the commission you are in a position to generate. A very attractive product on that front is life assurance which generates 5% of the assured capital in the event of death.

Commissions vary widely per product and will therefore encourage you to push certain products more than others. For example, the income on the sale of investment products is 4% if sold through an insurance company, 3% for equity funds, 2 % for bond funds, 0.5% for money market funds, 0.25% on the sale of individual shares.

Management fees vary between 0.15% and 2 %.

Those different levels of commission will thus have an immediate impact on the revenues of your branch and will of course be key parameters when establishing your "Sales Plan".

Example of a simplified sales plan.

Now that you know the key parameters which influence the revenues of your branch you can take it a step further and elaborate a plan such as briefly outlined hereafter.

SALES PLAN 2005

2004 Figures

REVENUES 2004 = 1.794.527

1.794.527 x 106% = 1.902.198

Ptf Revenues

Liabilities = 828.346

Assets = 626.881 - 89.024* = 537.857

* 89.024 represent the fees related to life assurance contract for STL in 2.004. The result from the total amount of premiums paid by the customers (136.960) multiplied by the rate of commission, i.e. 65%

Investments : 172.613

Total : 1.538.816

Gap = 1.902.198 (the objective for 2004) - 1.538.816 = 363.382€.

Those figures are from the previous period. The crunch is that it is difficult to influence these figures in the very short term and that the "spread" is fluctuating beyond your control.

Example of a goal setting for sales.

Life assurance: 1.000.000 EUR of assured capital = 50.000 € of revenues

Sale of investment products: 9.000.000 x 2.5% (average commission) = 225.000 EUR

ASRD 175.000 EURO = 113.750 EUR

TOTAL = 388.750 EURO

GOAL SETTINGS ON AN INDIVIDUAL LEVEL

Spreading of above mentioned goals per employee involved in sales

SPECIAL COMMERCIAL ACTIONS

A list of actions to be held at branch level to achieve above goals

Most banks will have nation-wide commercial actions managed from the central marketing department. Local branches can launch more tailor-made on the spot commercial actions, however, which will directly impact on expenses.

Overhead / Expenses

In this example overhead is computed on a central basis and charged to branches in proportion to their contribution to the overall balance sheet of the bank

Employee expense is computed on a central basis and allocated as a function of staff employed.

The approach described is a typical retailer's approach. A more conventional approach would be to have a branch taking care of its balance sheet at branch level along the same lines as the overall organisation. This would mean than that the overall balance sheet is the consolidated balance sheet of all the branches. Each branch in that case is run as a small independent bank. The accent would slightly shift from selling to cost versus revenue management.

Control and Audit

Corporate Values

The term business ethics refer to how an institution, a bank, a corporation, a business in general terms, integrates core values – such as honesty, trust, respect and fairness- into its policies, practices and decision making throughout all levels of the business.

Business ethics involves a bank's compliance with legal standards and its adherence to internal rules and regulations. Numerous companies of different sizes and sectors have demonstrated their commitment to developing ethical decision-making processes. The successful processes these companies have used to institutionalise ethical initiatives include, but are not limited to, mission statements, ethical principles or values statements, ethics officers, ethics communication strategies, ethics training and discussion groups, continuous evaluations, rewards and sanctions.

Whilst there is no commonly accepted definition of business **social responsibility,** the general view is that it is a set of policies, practices and programs that are integrated throughout business operations, and decision-making processes and which are rewarded and supported by top management[28].

Over the past decade, a growing number of companies has recognised the business benefits of social responsibility. Empirical studies have shown that it has a positive impact on performance, and is not harmful to shareholder value.

The value of social responsibility can be measured in a number of ways which include:

- financial performance,
- reduced operating cost,
- enhanced brand image and reputation,
- increased customer sales and customer loyalty,
- increased productivity and quality,
- increased ability to attract and retain employees,
- reduced regulatory oversight
- access to capital

This is maybe hard to believe? Do you remember a book, which was widely recognised, entitled: "In search of excellence"? The ingredients of excellence are everywhere in every single detail of the organisation but predominant in the mind of every single employee working for the organisation.

The "Caux Round Table"[29] has produced universal principles for ethical responsibilities. It is an interesting document, which seeks to express a world-wide standard for ethical and responsible business behaviour. The principles include the social impact of business operations on the local community, a respect of rules and ethics, support for multilateral trade agreements that promote the "judicious liberation of trade", respect for the environment and "avoidance of illicit operations", such as bribery, money laundering and corruption.

Implementation of this "attitude" is to be reflected in all parts of the business and obviously particularly at branch level.

---

28) Global Business responsibility resource centre at http://www.corporatecitizenship.net/business_ethics.html

29) Business for Social Responsibility is a US-based global resource for companies seeking to sustain their commercial success in ways that demonstrate respect for ethical values, for people, communities and the environment. http://www.cauxroundtable.org

Ethics

One of the files you will find on your desk on gaining access to
your manager's office is the procedures on ethics and corporate
values. It will in all likelihood not be your top priority. However,
as soon as you have settled in do take your time to look at it as
it is precisely in this field that losses are incurred. It is also a
corporate requirement.

Basic principles of ethics are almost universal in the financial sector.
Think about foreign exchange. It is an over the counter market with
substantial settlement risks for enormous amounts but it does work.
Look at the book of the code of conduct of the dealers' association. It
is quite substantial indeed. However as virtually everyone respects the
rules it allows for a "daily" turnover of about 2.000 billion €!

Management Background

**The basic principles of the banking sector
are summarised below** [30]

A bank should:

- *Serve customers diligently and loyally. Comply strictly with
  the duty of confidentiality and discretion in relation both to
  customers and to third parties*

- *Supply customers with useful information on the products and
  services offered and on the mutual commitments which these
  imply*

---

30) Code of Ethics of the Luxembourg Bank and Bankers' Association.

119

- *As a function of the services requested, seek information about the circumstances of the customer, his needs and his constraints*

- *Make sure that staff act honestly, in the best interest of the customers, the bank and the integrity of the market*

- *Endeavour to avoid conflicts of interest and, where such conflicts are inevitable, make sure that customers are treated equitably*

- *Have at its disposal, and make effective use of the resources and procedures necessary for the proper performance of its activities*

- *Make a clear distinction between its own assets and transactions and those of third parties*

- *Comply with the laws and regulations governing its activities and co-operate with the competent authority to see that they are properly applied*

- *Refrain from giving advice which may encourage misdemeanours and enter into no transactions involving funds accruing from criminal activity*

- *Ensure honest and decent presentation of its advertising*

Quality management

Why is quality so important in the financial services industry?

By the early 1990s it was possible for a consumer to conduct all of his financial business without using a traditional bank.

The very essence of quality is to be seen to be better than the competition. Quality leads to branding, which means a name and a reputation representing a single company and a single set of expectations. If quality is not part of the day to day line management and decision making at *all levels of the organization* it will dissipate or be sidelined by short term financial goals. Financial services companies need to build and manage brand loyalty. This relates to how and why a company promises to be different, how it behaves on delivering those promises. A promise and its delivery create a reputation or brand image. In order to achieve this goal, quality is an absolute must.

Factors such as changing customer needs, new technology, new regulations, downsizing and globalization have altered the power base and *outlook of customers and prospects, employees and the investment community,* and have raised the importance of branding. Banking has a heritage and culture of non-competition, which has resulted in branding being under-emphasised; it is now one of its most important assets. Marketing, hence quality, was less important in a regulated industry.

Quality is important more than ever as companies begin to compete across what used to be industry boundaries. Insurance companies, investment firms, credit card providers, software providers, information providers, such as AT&T, GE, GMAC, American, Sears, Safeway's are formidable forces competing to deliver financial services, often with smaller overheads! The number of possible providers grows rapidly and the exclusivity between the prospective provider and the customer diminishes.

Quality and reputation:
- They are not optional
- They set a level of expectations
- They set a level of associations
- They are the glue that holds together the substance of the company, what its products stand for & its employees
- They are a point of reference

"The benefits of branding are awareness, loyalty, *perceived quality* and creation of leveraged associations that are the crucial ingredients for survival & success." It also forces the institution to focus on the right customers and be more cost effective.

The goals that need to be achieved in order to reach outstanding quality are numerous: they include at least the following ingredients:
- Team building with respect of colleagues
- High standard of quality and professionalism
- Customer focus
- Mutual respect
- Goals start with each employee
- Integrity, courtesy & urgency
- The customer comes first
- Sharing success, rewards and failures
- Individual accountability (MBO)
- Professionalism
- A committment to high standards
- Knowledge
- Performance- and values measurement
- Relevant Training
- Establish credibility of the value system
- Consistency
- Uniformity in approach
- Discipline

The ultimate goal: is customer satisfaction

31) Richard H Evans in "Growing Brand Loyalty", Lafferty Publications

122

The musts for quality searches in different fields are as follows:

- Avoiding vagueness
- Continuity and consistency
- If need be altering perceptions
- Avoiding disharmony, which can lead to a loss of market share
- Avoiding fragmentation which limits focus
- Maintaining consistency & harmony in whatever is relevant to the company such as names, logo, colour, messages.
- Functional harmony within the various lines of business
- Individual key performance measures
- Shared goals throughout the corporation
- Financial performance measurement throughout the corporation

Why is this all so important?

The customer will remember you. He feels he is being well treated. He feels important to the organisation. He feels that his needs are met, that he has value for money.

What are the results of quality?

The branch will be considered as professional! Of all the compliments one can receive this is the best one, it says it all.

Risk management

Right now, the financial services industry is at a turning point. There has grown up an intensely competitive culture in which every established practice now has to be questioned, as if each institution and structure were starting again from scratch. Management is focusing on cost and profits as never before.

In our part of the world, we are probably heading towards the end of a secure comfortable existence. Indeed, employers are transferring much of the natural uncertainty of economic life to those who used to be called employees. The accent on share price performance grows stronger, partly as a result of the rapid development of the fund management industry.

On top of all this, the economic and social environment is changing as well, showing:
- an ageing population,
- more single parents,
- time as an increased scarce resource,
- fewer safety nets,
- home based business,
- technologically astute customers,
- a growing income gap,
- a rising small business sector

The assessment and handling of risk is the most challenging part of the banking industry which faces four major challenges, of which the risk challenge is but one. Risk can be broken down into about twenty categories such as:

- Liquidity risk
- Interest rate risk
- Capital risk
- Credit risk
- Cost risk
- Market risk
- Foreign exchange and settlement risk
- Off balance sheet risk
- Technological and operational risk
- Country and sovereign risk
- Macro-economic risk
- Legal risk
- Loss of reputation risk (often referred to as "reputation risk")

> *Money laundering is directly linked to the "reputation risk".*

The responsibility of risk management is a matter for everyone, not just specialists

Risk management is subject to a code of conduct and is a matter of education. Sounds familiar, doesn't it? Risk management is a matter of permeating the branch's structure with an awareness of risks. Vital in this whole process is the application of human and technical resources. Training in this instance is essential. Learn to spot anything unusual, anything incoherent and anything well outside the norm. As stated earlier, this can easily be achieved by systems of customer segmentation and profiling.

"Implementing a management framework which defines roles and responsibilities and involves all the functions of the bank requires experience, knowledge and impartiality. Information is a key to it all"[32]. In this field as in many others, the difference between banks will be a matter of software. The challenge will be to supply adequate information "in a concise manner" and based on highlighting exceptions in order to provide a better overall visibility, anticipate problems and control high risk operations.

"The key factors to successful risk-management are:
- The involvement of the entire branch
- Obtaining the interactivity between the organisation and systems
- Designing an integrated computing architecture with a high level of interactivity with risk oriented systems
- Extracting consistent information.
- A coherent organisation of the branch for effective risk management
- Favouring a horizontal approach to obtain a risk picture for the whole bank
- A clear statement of management as to the goals to achieve and the responsibilities.[33]"

---

32) Conference: "An introduction to risk management" by Mr. Yvon Lauret, Banque Internationale, Luxembourg

33) Mr. Y. Lauret, op.cit.

Compliance

Compliance is the responsibility of ensuring that the various businesses of an institution remain fit and proper in accordance with all regulatory requirements applicable to the financial sector.

In general, compliance officers are in charge of the following items[34]:

- Bank secrecy or discretion (indeed few countries know the concept of bank secrecy enshrined in the legal code).
- Customer and employee data protection
- Money laundering prevention and 'know your customer'
- Insider dealing
- Employees' fraud
- Retention of documents
- Conflict of interest / Chinese walls
- Ethical policies / Code of conduct
- Reporting to local regulators
- Employee training on compliance
- Compliance with internal policies and procedures
- Compliance with local banking regulations and market practices
- Business specific regulatory requirements
- (Potential) Sanctions

Compliance is not of the sole remit of the Compliance function. Indeed, compliance with the rules applicable to the institutions is also a matter for the board of directors, senior management, as well as staff members, and is thereby to be considered as a key element of the **compliance culture of a branch**.

---

34) Mr. Fabrice Blondé of Citigroup, conference on Measures against Money Laundering, Luxembourg

Bank secrecy

Is the result of two sets of considerations:

- Its justification lies in the respect for public order
- It provides indispensable confidence and privacy

However rules for lifting secrecy are there in order to avoid possible misuses of too strict a secrecy obligation. Indeed, bank secrecy rules have been amended in various countries mainly because of three significant developments:

- Ever increasing fiscal crime
- Ever increasing financial speculation
- Money laundering from illegal activities, such as sales of drugs.

Therefore, during the last decade many countries introduced exceptions to the rules in relation to money laundering. The financial sector lost its immunity and set a trend for a series of measures.

It should be pointed out that bank secrecy is automatically lifted in the case of money laundering in countries with bank secrecy such as Switzerland or Luxembourg. Bank secrecy is lifted in the case of money laundering. On that front, the best defence against money laundering remains a thorough knowledge of the customer, not just his identification but the reason for the relationship, the origin of the funds, the likely transactions, etc. It is a marketing requirement anyway to know the customer as well as possible, bet it only to maximise the opportunities for cross selling.

Employees' fraud

Confidential information and security are clearly linked to "authorised communications" either with customers or with the authorities. Leaks are not acceptable and can happen very easily: be they verbal or physical or computer related.[35] As far as money laundering is concerned the guideline should be quite clear: Nobody can release information about suspicions relative to a customer with the exception of the compliance officer.

The compliance officer can only release information to the relevant authority, which ideally should be the public prosecutor (or authorities), who is equally bound by professional secrecy.

In this context 'customer' is understood to be the account signature holder but equally the co-account holder, acting on his own account or on behalf of third parties, his agents and representatives, family, friends, auditors and heirs, the economic beneficiary.

Information leaks are quite common and may be malicious. They may be intentional or even unintentional. Worse would be an abuse of position by an inside or outside person acting with malice. This is the worst form of fraud.

Fraud can happen in the form of loss or theft of documents, from a counter, a desk or a briefcase. It can obviously also happen through burglary, theft of files or listings. Much more common nowadays is the theft of diskettes, listings, screen prints not to speak of hacking into internet, telephone-banking, and other similar distribution channels. Leaks represent both an internal as well as an external risk factor.

What can we do about it? Here too, we would provide the same answer as for money laundering issues. How is the institution organised? How are logistics controlled in your branch?

• **Organisation**

There is a need to identify and select highly sensitive information and examine the best way of organising such matters within the bank in order to avoid the risk of leakage of confidential data. Relevant structures and procedures should be in place.

---

35) Mess. R. Greden and PP Boegen, Expertise Patrimoniale, Luxembourg in a course on "Evaluation of staff risk in financial institutions".

- **Logistics**

There is a need to identify physical activities such as maintenance, security, technical operations and to analyse the related risk. Security rules should be established to avoid liabilities emanating from high-risk activities.

- **Information technology**

Fraud in this field has overtaken more traditional forms of fraud. An absolute must is ensuring security at user level as well as at management level let alone at customer level.

Fraud is often the result of human behaviour surfacing as a result of unconscious needs, severe frustration or just criminal activities. Most organisations experience frustrated employees for all sorts of reasons.

Therefore the branch manager should consider the environment and atmosphere in which employees work. Furthermore he should remain alert to behaviour which indicate frustration.

The Chinese Wall

In most branches today the operational part has been centralised in regional or notional centres making branches less prone to have conflicts of interest between the commercial and the operational side of the branch. It is a sound principle to split tasks so that one person never has the power to conclude a transaction on his own.

Tasks should be split and dual signatures and confirmations by a different department required. This splitting of duty is cast in stone and is one of the basic principles of prudence, hence the reason why it has been called the Chinese wall.

For those who have had the chance to see the wall, I guess they will agree that it is so impressive that it is almost beyond belief. The same should be said concerning potential errors in the branch.

Filing

Control starts with filing. Often when an internal audit team randomly audits the branch network, the first thing they will do after sealing off the branch is to examine the filing. A well organised branch has a well organised filing system. Nothing is more time consuming than looking for ill filed documents. Make sure every employee and every department follows exactly the same methodology.

In order to achieve 100% efficiency in this field, every branch in the system should have the same methodology. Work with key words, colours, often needed files or seldom needed files, files under double custody, files for archives. Whatever your choice, make sure it is identical for all involved. Also, make sure your files are frequently reviewed so that only what is useful is filed. Send out of date filing to the archives, which should be filed using the same logic as the often used files.

Filing is part of marketing as well. What impression will your customers, both external and internal, take away when they come into a branch which looks messy and into your office which does not look at all tidy? They may conclude that your actions will match the image and a potential income will be lost.

Assess each document for its relevance.

Monitoring Progress

Control should not be rigid to the point where it discourages people from working freely. However, start from the point of view that you have to monitor even when you know tasks are in good hands. It does not mean that you are going to intervene very often but you should not be caught unaware. If something goes wrong it will affect your career as well as your branch's rating.

Monitoring will also help your thinking. It will highlight where certain functions need to be improved. Even if you do not have the authority within your branch to change procedures or processes, the fact you are thinking about it and looking for improvement or greater efficiency can only help you. It will help problems to be anticipated as much as possible and avoided rather than solved when the damage has been done.

IF things go wrong, think positively, look for solutions to prevent reoccurrence Find out why things went wrong. Analyse all the facts including your own instructions or delegation structure. Consider the implications of possible amendments to the system or to the areas of responsibility.

> *Tip: In case of fraud or concealment, take punitive action immediately and in case of excellence also reward immediately!*

Audit

Smaller branches may not have an audit function. Larger branches would have an independent audit unit, which should closely co-ordinate its activities with the audit department of the institution.

Audit is as an important a function as marketing. It can be a powerful tool for change and for achievement of excellence. Auditing like marketing is a driver of change. Control is there to make sure all is done according to specified procedures, whereas audit has a further dimension, either by recommending procedures or by reviewing existing procedures in order to improve on the activities of the organisation.

Audit is also a check on the interval between good ideas and their execution, called the execution gap. Audit is of help in the effort to improve on customer profitability as well as to minimise cost.

Audit can best intervene in establishing:

- New benchmarks

- Establishing best practices

- Establishing best procedures per distribution channel

The sales process

Selling is essential to business, but not only to business, also to you as a person. Your goal is to gain agreement from others. So, in fact you are selling much more than you think. An example, you want to go to the theatre tonight and your partner prefers to go swimming. One of the two of you will have to be a better salesperson than the other one. Imagine, you would like to have a promotion to a larger branch! There you are again: selling!

Here too, think like an entrepreneurial retailer. The primary goal is to increase sales but the long term goal is to create a relationship.

"An understanding of how and why customers choose between suppliers, combined with good sales disciplines, offers the best hope for increasing revenue from new and existing customers".

The initial contact with the customer

Imagine yourself being stopped by a police officer, who criticises you for driving well beyond the authorised speed limit.

Roughly speaking, you have two possibilities.

- Either you tell him: «I really am in a hurry and I have more important things to do than this». As the saying goes, "you rub him up the wrong way". You can guess the consequence. He will in all likelihood do some further checking, taking as much time as he possibly can.

- Alternatively, you tell him: "I am ever so sorry. I have probably been a bit absent minded…" This time you rub him up the right way. With a bit of luck he will tell you that you ought to pay attention and that «It is OK on this occasion».

> We all have three levels of communication:
> - → The parent
> - → The adult
> - → The child

The police officer talks to you as a parent and really expects you to react and reply as a child. If you talk to him as an adult, or even worse as a parent, it will not meet his expectations and your approach may cost you quite a lot. An adult to adult relationship is a parallel relationship. «Isn't it a beautiful day, today?» «Yes, indeed.» These are non-conflicting adult sentences.

An appropriate type of transaction is, for example: The branch manager who tells an associate that the desks should be cleared every evening, upon which the employee would answer "Yes, of course sir, I'll make sure it is done punctually." This would be a harmonious parent child transaction whereby the employee recognises the authority of the branch manager and acts accordingly.

36) Branch Profitability, David Cavell, Lafferty Publications, Ireland

136

Parent	Parent
Adult	Adult
Child	Child

Needless to say it is an absolute requirement to be on the same wavelength before commencing a dialogue. **The initial contact with the customer follows the same principle.** In terms of selling it means the first step: do your homework so that you know the background and the circumstances before you do anything further.

The customer buying process

Marketing has analysed the buyer so thoroughly that there are few mysteries left. The buying process leads the customer through a series of buying steps. Each step reflects how the customer feels at various stages of the relationship as the selling process advances. At each step, there is a strategy that enables the salesperson to help the customer advance to the point of effective conclusion.

The classical steps are from no interest at all to:

♦ Low interest where the customer listens

♦ Strong interest where the customer explores, looks at alternatives, questions

♦ Relatively convinced where the customer is looking closely at price aspects, delivery mode, etc

♦ Closing with the salesperson's intention to follow up after the sales

Objections

Objections should be viewed as opportunities. Getting the answers relative to the objections is part of the selling process:

♦ They allow you to educate the customer

♦ They allow you to gain information from the customer

♦ They are the proof that the customer is interested

♦ They give the opportunity, if handled well, to convince and close the transaction

37) The analysis on the basis of those models is called the "Transactional Analysis"

Objections should be regarded as a wall of bricks, which you have to knock down. Thus do it brick per brick. Treat objections with great care and handle them one by one. Ideally you should know the objections you might encounter. In any event, you will be able to address any possible questions more readily if you have responses prepared in advance.

Needless to say, practice is the best coach. Do not bank on intuition, inborn sales skills, feeling, bank rather on know how, methodology, logic and discipline in your presentation. Remember to listen, listen and listen. Selling is like flying an aeroplane, it is a matter of hours of flying.

Tip: You will be able to handle most of the objections but never try to convince someone who acts on Principles. You might succeed in convincing them but it will take you much more time than is at your disposal in a sales dialogue. For that reason, do not be afraid, like pilots to fly with two people. This will allow you to check each other and complement each other. Two heads always think about more issues than one head. It will improve your ability to advance the discussion and the argumentation and be ready for customer objections more effectively. It will also allow for mutual feedback and allow for corrective actions straight away. Remember this obsession with detail and this permanent goal of achieving an outstanding performance.

Perceptions

People perceive things "on the surface" along the same lines. In fact they often perceive things in a fundamentally different way than you might expect. It is up to the salesperson to close the gap between the customer's perception and the real characteristics of the service proposed. Do not assume all is clear or clearly known. Therefore, regular summaries in the framework of the sales dialogue are a must. Make sure there is no gap between the facts and what the customer "perceives" as facts. An example in the field of investments: After having listened quite a long while to your explanation on the various types of funds, the customer tells you "I know enough about mutual funds and there is never a loss of capital!" You have just explained the various types of funds! This gap very, very often happens and leads to misunderstanding or unsatisfied customers!

The damage done could be substantial and in any event it would be another drain on available time, which should be avoided.

Customer styles

The analysis of a customer's situation is closely interrelated with the client's style.

In a traditional sale, one recognises usually four quite different styles:

ACTION	Individuals who speak with authority, who are result driven, jump quickly to conclusions, are stress-resistant, with a focused mind and a sense of follow-up. They are often impatient and are often convinced about the correctness of their point of view.
ANALYSIS	Individuals who often speak with knowledge, in a reserved manner, who analyse a problem in a systematic way and who, above all, look for quality and security. They often have too great a sense of detail and are also often very critical.
HARMONY	Individuals who speak with respect and with a sense of purpose in order to find a mutually satisfactory solution. They are quite positive and if need be will accept compromises. They are often too tolerant and too dependent upon the esteem of the others.
AFFECTIVE	Individuals who show great respect for others. They are often intuitive and creative. They weather problems easily and are happy when they find a solution. They often take far too much time over one issue and are easily side-tracked and loose sight of their objective.

It is up to the salesperson to adjust to the customer's style.

We can also segment people according to their investor profile. It is an essential segmentation in Private Banking. This segmentation is probably more useful than the one we have just been examining. Anyway, please note that human communication is a complex issue and that every crossroad may generate a misunderstanding.

In «Private Banking» we have learned that a handful of focused questions need to be asked in order to get a decent idea of the investor's profile.

The nature of the answers to the questions will allow us to propose an appropriate product in line with the needs of the customer, in other words appropriate to his appetite for risk.

For example, an individual with a lot of relevant experience, relatively young, without need of liquidity who is investing only a modest portion of his assets (which are quite significant) and whose objective is capitalisation rather than distribution, will receive an investment proposal allocating most of his assets to shares with very few to bonds.

Whatever the profile of the customer, let us keep in mind the following 7 points:

1st   In the final analysis, the customer pays our salary or our commission.

2nd   The customer does not depend on us we depend on him.

3rd   The customer does not interrupt our workload; we work for the customer.

4th   The customer, who sees his problem being solved, gets what he is entitled to; we are not doing him a favour.

5th   The customer is part of our net worth.

6th   The customer is not an account number.

7th   The customer is the rationale for the branch

Contacting customers by telephone

We can consider various sorts of segmentation of the customers:

- Segmentation as to attitude in dialogue: parent, adult and child

- Segmentation as to the nature of the communication: action, analysis, harmony and affective

- Segmentation as to the investor's profile: taking a smaller or greater amount of risk

It is certainly interesting; but what happens on the telephone?

You do not have the benefit of body language, which represents 50% of communication. You do not have the benefit of information regarding the style of the customer; maybe you do not even have his investor profile to hand. You often do not have time nor even the opportunity to listen properly.

However, that very telephone call is "the" link between the customer and your institution. If everything goes well, you will have a happy customer who, in all likelihood, will talk about it. If you leave an unhappy customer, he will certainly talk about it to friends and relatives.

This telephone call, like all others, is essential for:
- The reputation of the bank
- To maintain excellence
- Your reputation
- Your career
- Your commercial and operational objectives
- Your ego
- Your personal satisfaction
- (You can probably add quite a few other reasons)

This very telephone call needs to be a tone-setter in customer contact, in service and in commercial approach. It is your and your institution's business card. The quality of that very telephone call is significant and essential for every one in the organisation.

Quality does exist. Quality depends on:

- Your attitude
- Your methodology
- Your sensitivity to the customer's profile
- Your attitude as to the number of times you let the telephone ring before answering
- Your first sentences
- The way you introduce yourself
- The way you create an atmosphere
- The way you LISTEN

The listening and selling technique

LISTENING

Start with active listening (the opposite of absentminded listening) and whilst not doing a thousand and one things at the same time. Confucius[38] stated that we have two ears and one mouth in order to listen twice as much as we speak. Seneca[39] added wisely that one should only break a silence if one has something meaningful to say. Additionally, if you make a statement, the customer might object to your comments.

Do not make statements unless absolutely required. Do ask questions instead.

QUESTIONS

Do ask questions rather than make statements. A question translates interest, attention. A question is never stupid; answers may be. It is by means of open and closed questions that you will enable the customer

38) Confucius: author and philosopher in China (a.551-479 ante J.C.). His philosophy is moral and political.

39) Seneca: Latin author (Cordoba a.60 ante. J.C - Rome a.39 post J.C) author of the "Controversies", which is a precious document on the oratory art during the first century.

to express his problem and his expectations clearly. Unless you ask sufficient questions, you run the risk of proposing a solution, which may not be in line with his expectations.

THE STRUCTURE

Please remember the structure of effective selling:

Situation: What is the situation of the customer? Who is he? In which segment might he be?

⇓

Problem: Why is he calling? What is his concern? Is it urgent? Are we talking about an administrative or a commercial issue? Is it a matter of interpretation or of comprehension?

⇓

Information: Does the client have all the required information to define his problem? Does the client understand the nature of the error or the reason for the lack of communication? Handle objections one by one!

⇓

Solution: Does the customer understand what needs to be done? Does he really understand the benefit of the proposed solution?

Questions – Questions – Questions

If the customer does not understand why you are asking so many questions, explain the reason for doing so. The reason is that you want to arrive at the optimal solution in line with his expectations.

In the event that your question is not clear to him, ask another question in order to clarify the first one.

THE ATTITUDE

Contrary to common belief, the person at the other end of the telephone will sense your attitude. The person will sense if his or her problem is not attracting your concern. The person will know if you are sweet or ill-tempered. A positive and constructive attitude, reflected by your questions, highlight a professional attitude.

143

Please note that your attitude will already be evident by the number of times you let the telephone ring before answering! ! ! Ideally, the telephone should not ring more than three times.

PRESENTATION

The first seconds are the most important ones. At that very moment, you are selling your image and the image of your institution. This, the consumer's first impression will be quite difficult to modify later.

You have to earn the right to ask questions! You have to gain sympathy! That is the reason why it is appropriate to pick up the telephone quickly and to present oneself in the same way others do in the organisation.

An example: « EDG-Bank, First Name + Name, Good Morning» and wait. Learn to wait. Let the customer talk to you do not hurry. Listen!

And if the client says nothing? Simple, just say: «How can I help you? ».

IDENTIFICATION

Remember the first phase of a sale is the situation: Who is my counterpart?

Try to segment the customer as soon as possible thanks to the initial data that he gives you, such as an account number plus any other data that you can elicit from him which will help you to place him. Use his name to show that you know him, or at least that you have recognised him.

Do not forget that the customer expects to be the centre of your attention. A lack of proper identification or interest on your part will immediately and irrevocably penalise you.

THE ANALYSIS OF THE TELEPHONE CALL

Your questions will have enabled the customer to determine the exact nature of his problem. Do not refrain from reformulating his problem in order to ascertain that you are indeed on the same wavelength and to ensure that you are in a position to fulfil the customer's expectations.

In the event that expectations are not realistic, make sure you explain why this is the case and ensure that you review what should be done about it, highlighting relevant advantages and disadvantages of the alternative solution.

EXPECTATIONS

The telephone is not free. Do not keep a customer waiting on the telephone. If the waiting time is short, tell him why he may have to wait a "short" time. If this time is longer than very short: call back!

At all costs avoid "Just a moment" which lasts an eternity, even more so if the customer is in a hurry or is in a bad mood. Calling back means that you are working on the customer's problem. Additionally, it leaves you some time to search for relevant information or to discuss about the customer's expectations with one of your colleagues.

THE CONCLUSION

The conclusion needs to be crystal-clear for all parties involved. If need be rephrase the conclusion to ascertain all is clear. If the customer cannot make up his mind or find the right solution, ask closed questions. He or she will have to answer with a yes or a no. This will enable you to advance towards the final solution.

TRANSFERRING THE COMMUNICATION

A critical moment! To refer the customer to the wrong departement is damaging for your image.

Losing the connection is equally bad. Make sure the transfer has indeed happened to the right person and the right department. Make sure the customer has found as professional a counterpart as you are.

THE LANGUAGE

Please remember that we all represent a certain type of individual. Besides, we all have a parent, an adult and a child in us. Do not offend your customer. We are not saying that the customer is always right but it is up to us, as professionals, to master a technique. By means of focused questions, it is up to us to show that we are professionals. For this reason we need, at least at the very beginning to talk the language of the customer.

PROFESSIONAL

The best compliment you can receive is "Thank you, very professional". This is a pleasing confirmation of the customer's appreciation that the service has been in line with his expectations. A precise and effective answer to customers' expectations is the "ABC" in marketing. Please keep in mind the numerous challenges banks face in order to survive.

TIME

Nothing takes "five minutes". Call the customer back if you know that you will only be listening with half an ear (whereas we have two). When you cannot spare the required time, undertake to call back soonest. Make a note that you have a call to return. Do call back, no matter what.

Summarising, the structure of a phone call is as follows:

Ring

⇓

Presentation

⇓

Identification

⇓

Questions

⇓

Reformulation

⇓

Supplementary questions

⇓

Time for eventual research/ call back

⇓

Information

⇓

Constructive formulation of the problem and its solution

⇓

Isolation of every objection and point by point argumentation

⇓

Conclusion by means of closed questions

⇓

Thank the customer for his trust and express the wish to help him in the future

Mastering delicate situations

Undoubtedly, you will have noticed that technique is not superfluous in the field of communication. The more structured you are the more chance you will have of reaching a solution to the satisfaction of all involved.

In the event of a situation being difficult due to intrinsic features of the problem, or because of the obvious irritation of the customer, or even because of his very subjective approach which borders on insulting you:

«Relax!» You are not being blamed personally.

Take the attitude of a person who is resolving a problem for two other parties: the customer on one side and the supplier on the other. You are not part of the problem. You are trying to resolve it.

You are looking for a solution in the capacity of a consultant.

Be a professional consultant. This implies that you will be systematic, structured, with a clear-cut objective and providing a service of such a quality that you will stay in the picture for future jobs as well. In the future, you will be the one who will be required to take on a new challenge.

> *The technique is the same for all sorts of sales:*
> *Listening ⇒ Analysing ⇒ Summarising ⇒ Informing ⇒*
> *Questioning in order to conclud**e***

The customer is neither always wrong, nor always right. It does not really matter. What matters is that you are a professional in a position to satisfy the customer. Remember that you are the best advertising for the branch. Besides, a satisfied customer will talk about you to other potential customers.

Likewise in this case: ask questions. Avoid statements even more than usual. Avoid everything which might worsen the already complicated situation. It is up to you to master the situation. Avoid at all costs giving the impression that the problem is not your concern. Avoid stating who is right or wrong. That is not the problem. You need to reach a definite goal. That is the only thing which matters really; not what you think, nor what you feel! You want to achieve that very goal in a professional way and with a high degree of integrity.

The attitudes of wisdom

Let us start with a bit of advice, which has already appeared in the course.

The most significant piece of advice is undoubtedly from Seneca: « Only speak if you have something significant to say».

Let us also remember the sentence from Confucius: «We have two ears and only one mouth in order to listen twice as much as we speak».

- Do not make statements. Rather, ask questions.
- A question is never stupid, only an answer may be.
- A customer's complaint needs to be seen as an opportunity
- A human being has not the patience to listen, therefore he prefers judging!
- He who commits an error without putting it right, commits a second one!

Even more:

- Always take objections very seriously
- Be conscious of your attitude
- Isolate each objection and address them one by one
- Always finish a conversation on a positive note
- See the matter through; do not leave any doubt as to courses of action to be taken by the parties involved.
- Conclude with closed questions (yes or no).

Do not forget that even when there is no visual contact, the customer senses your attitude, your state of mind, your willingness to conclude the transaction to everyone's satisfaction. For example, a smile whilst you are calling will be sensed at the other end of the line and will improve communication. The other party will feel your dynamism almost instinctively. Take the opportunity to ask questions which lead to a solution not unlike a funnel leading to an exit, a solution.

In the absence of visual contact, one needs to be even more precise. Use simple short sentences. Avoid evasive answers: the credibility of yourself and your employer is at stake. Do not use negative phrases;

they will be detrimental to the effectiveness of your technique and above all the conclusion.

Remember: «What matters is concluding!»

From a constructive point of view, a customer's complaint represents an opportunity. An error will have to be corrected. Who is faultless? In this particular case, the appropriate attitude for solving the problem will enable you to keep the customer and to make him realise that he is dealing with a professional.

Please keep in mind the statistics from a retail bank relative to customers' complaints.

◆ To start with, only 5 % of customers react angrily.

◆ In the event of a complaint being unresolved, 10% of customers stay with the organisation whereas 90% quit.

◆ In the event that there is no entirely satisfactory solution, 20% stay and 80% quit.

◆ In the event that there is a fully satisfactory solution, 30 to 50% stay whereas 50 to 30% quit.

Furthermore, think about the marketing aspect of the complaint. That very complaint is a significant piece of information. It might highlight human errors, system errors, errors of comprehension or communication, an unclear procedure, etc. These factors need to be registered and followed-up in order to prevent their recurrence. One may commit an error but not the same one twice! ! !

A few more tips

❏ Never be on the defensive, you are a consultant who is seeking a mutually acceptable solution.

❏ Never be critical. You are a professional. The only acceptable criticism is constructive criticism.

❏ Only promise what you can deliver

❏ Never take things personally, there is a difference between the professional and you as a private person.

❏ Learn from each situation as much as you can; knowledge means survival.

You are selling all the time

When you write a report or a memorandum, you are selling. Keep in mind the basics:

1) What is the issue

2) What is the proposal

3) What information is needed to reach a conclusion

4) A recommendation

It is no different from selling! Always follow up. Again this is selling. Do not forget to interrogate yourself as to the reasons why people might disagree with you and what arguments you could use to break down their point of view. Is this not selling? Also remember the basics of marketing in selling, which tells us that there is a "pre-selling" phase before you actually sell!

Other questions to ask yourself: about cost, of course. What is this proposal going to cost and how much income is it going to generate. What are the marketing implications? What is going to be lost if the branch or the bank does not implement your recommendation? What are the ingredients of success?

A recent survey in the UK retail banking sector underlined that over 70% of the retail banking buyers stated that their preference was not for "hard selling –product pushing- but for reputation, service, experience and purchase convenience (the revenue drivers). In addition excessive emphasis on selling decreases motivation of staff and detracts from revenue drivers and customer retention[40].

40) David Cavell, "Branch Profitability", Lafferty Publications

Franchising

Franchising has been successfully applied in many service industries. Obviously, the best known is McDonalds but there are many other examples such as Hilton, Mister Minute, Speedy, and in Belgium Citibank and Dexia, with many franchised branches.

Franchising means that the owner of the business, in this case the branch, is the **franchisee**, i.e. the branch manager. He runs the branch in the true sense of an entrepreneur and often owns the premises. He is entirely responsible for the profit and loss account of this business. So he is no different to other entrepreneurs. He receives from the **franchisor** the full support of a central marketing department, product development and product support as well as systems assistance.

One talks about a contract between two businesses, whereby the franchiser grants distribution rights in a defined territory but on condition that the franchisee surrenders significant freedom as to how business is being conducted. The contractual terms will cover brands, pricing, product offering, systems, etc.

Credit decisions and credit exposure, which is definitely the biggest risk, is often taken over by the franchiser, who in that case makes the credit decisions based on the data collected by the franchisee, according to well established procedures and guidelines.

The main **advantage** is that the franchisee will certainly think like an entrepreneur, as he is one in the true sense of the word. Cost effectiveness will be his obsession as the expenses are his expenses and profits are the profits of his business. The second main advantage is continuity of personnel from the customers' viewpoint. In many financial services companies, job rotation is a fact for whatever reason. Continuity in a customer relationship is a goal of the organisation rather than a fact of life. A franchisee stays in the picture as it is his business and the customers are his customers.

Another advantage is that the various franchisees can cater better for the divergent needs of their respective customer bases. Take, as an example, Belgium, where in one country, three languages are spoken and where there is an attitude difference between north and south.

The franchisees will be much closer to their customer base and will make the difference. This might not necessarily be the case with branch managers who are promoted from one place to another.

A must is a strong central marketing department! It is a prerequisite as the franchisee's profit and loss depends upon the quality of the franchiser's propositions as to products, service, know how, market penetration, etc.

It is a formula, which is based on a strong mutual interdependence. It favours what we call the "bottom up" approach, i.e. the marketing and the systems will retrieve intelligence from the field, which is often not the case in traditional organisations where 'top down' is still pretty much the rule in strategic planning, for example.

There is a need for strong branding. There is a need for recognition, colours, and logos, which ascertain that despite differences from one franchised branch to another, they are part of the same group. Therefore, the integration will be more than cosmetic. There will be clearly binding rules, regulations and procedures as well as frequent control and audits.

Systems, especially in financial services, i.e. dealing with people's money, needs to be waterproof. Therefore, besides procedures, there will be a strict code of conduct and there should be **a law** on franchising to protect both the franchiser and the franchisee. Indeed, problems may easily occur that could bring the relationship between both into jeopardy. For instance, the franchiser might impose unattainable objectives, put the franchisee under pressure, and ultimately withdraw the franchising right.

The system also requires a certain flexibility as to the product range. In Belgium for instance most bank branches also sell insurance products, which are not necessarily from the franchiser. The same goes for investment products. Citibank and Deutsche bank in Belgium are large distributors of investment funds from the competition besides being distributors of their own in-house funds.

In fact this is quite a notable and successful approach to the market. It means: "our funds are fine but there are some better funds with the competition and we suggest you purchase those". The customer would find out anyway so he appreciates your frankness and this way you build up a relationship!

153

The problem with the franchisee is that he is often on the thin side as far as personnel are concerned. Procedures will see to it that a minimum of staff is required, which can be achieved by flying squads but at the expense of the franchisee.

The weak points of this type of organisation mean that a good legal framework is required. Indeed it is quite easy for a franchiser to withdraw the franchising right by imposing unattainable demands on the franchisee or imposing so many criteria for which the franchisee is liable to pay.

The franchise set up requires even more procedures than say a branch operation because the legal structure is at arms length. Fraud could be an increased danger and therefore more stringent controls and audit are required than in normal circumstances.

In a large organisation the corporate culture and corporate values are shared by all employees. Here there is a constellation of various quite different small enterprises, run very independently from each other. There might also be a conflict of interest as to the products being sold, for instance related to the level of the commissions earned on the various products. Therefore, certain franchisers ban all products other than their own branded products from being sold.

The tough issues are the discussions on the commissions and the annual targets! Commissions are pretty much in the hands of the franchiser in addition to the goals which need to be reached in order to enable the franchisee to retain his contract. Tough negotiations!

The key here, as you will have read, is the ownership of the business. The branch manager is no longer an employee-entrepreneur but an owner-entrepreneur. This requires more talent, imagination, local initiative and local knowledge of the exact customer base and its needs. Equally, it requires more motivation from branch employees who need to be aware that their future is in their own hands which should push them to perform not just for their job but for their survival.

One can certainly say that, in general, franchising has had a major impact on the profitability of branches. Branches now are leaner, more efficient, cost less to run and are more responsive to the customer base than the traditional branches. Furthermore the franchised branches have been made more aware of the need to push the customer towards cheaper distribution channels and free up time and space for advisory services.

Central ownership of branches is certainly easier from a legal and managerial point of view but often they have been inefficiently run and have therefore led banks to close branches rather than transforming them into efficient sales outlets.

Finally, franchising is about a different type of management, i.e. the management style of an entrepreneur, which we should all possess anyway, irrespective of whether the branch manager is an employee or a franchisee!

Setting up a new branch

It is strange to raise this issue but retail banking becomes retailing in the true sense of the word! It is true that in the EU a lot of banks opened branches in every village rather following the herd. In certain villages in Belgium for instance, there are more bank branches than shops.

Once the initial enthusiasm was over, banks started to realise that the branches were so expensive that certain organisations started to close them or merge them. With the advent of the new distribution channels and the virtual institutions yet more branches were closed. Now, we realise that customers are not yet ready to abandon the branch. They are back in fashion albeit in a different form!

Indeed the old traditional branch is gradually being replaced by a modern, attractive lay out combining the various functions of a modern retail outlet, as a result of market research.

Business Development

Undoubtedly the most difficult thing is the acquisition of new customers. You are not the only one attempting this. Targeting is done through TV, direct mail, clubs, social events, sponsoring, you name it. The local branch is heavily dependant upon the central marketing department and the quality of its advertising, logo, colours etc, i.e. the branding of the institution. The better the brand is known the easier is the initial approach for business development. However, once you have a foot in the door, the difference is no longer the branding but yourself! It is up to you!

We have noticed that it is an illusion to think that customers are customers of an organisation. They are customers of employees of an organisation and establish personal relationships. We have often seen in "private banking", for instance, that when a relationship manager leaves the bank, quite a few customers leave with the relationship manager. The statement is obvious but the best advertising is "word of mouth". If you and your staff are excellent customers will tell their relatives. It is the best investment you can make. So here we are back to excellence, marketing! It is a way of thinking and of doing business which is self-fulfilling.

Be particularly careful with inquiries from potential new customers. A failure at that stage is a disaster. Another potential disaster is when the sales person starts selling without listening, back to excellence… or without proper product knowledge, back to excellence!

You see the best thing for business development is excellence, not just from time to time but all day and every day. The biggest challenge for a branch manager is to achieve excellence day after day after day.

Business development will have to take into account the following clear trends in the financial services industry:

- Make the branch look like a smart outlet
- Organise the branch physically so that it looks different to others but functions in line with the services it sells
- The profit and loss will have to stand on its own merits
- Optimise use of new and diverse channels

Now, we always talk about attracting new customers but what about existing customers? You can:

- Cross-sell
- Upgrade existing relationships by suggesting improved or new products
- Handle telephone enquiries of existing customers with great diligence
- Send product information
- Invite customers to product presentations
- Analyse the account statements
- Provide free counselling
- Invite customers to social events
- Make joint calls with specialists
- Try to meet your customer base in local clubs, professional associations, community activities

But most of all, you attract new customers and deepen existing relationships by extending an impeccable service.

Cross selling

One often believes that the acquisition of new customers is the key to success. A survey in a Belgian Bank has shown that if a customer uses one product the gross average return to the bank is Euro 150 whereas if the customer purchases two products, the gross average return is Euro 450. Thus you need two new customers to get to the same result as selling one additional product to an existing customer!

Conclusion

As you will have realised, branch management boils down to people management and performance management . People require the right manager, who is a person with numerous qualities, as you have read. He should be alert to people's needs, ethical, respectful, flexible, ambitious, knowledgeable, …Difficult to find all those expected qualities but worth your while working on them as it impacts on your own performance, the performance of your colleagues, the performance of your branch and ultimately the performance of the institution you are working for.

Performance means return, productivity, organisation, control, quality, marketing, product knowledge, selling; also a long list of expectations, all up to you to achieve!

We have heard many times during training sessions: "this is not possible over here" or "that idea is never going to work" or "maybe in your country but not in mine". We often make the point that the trend in the financial services industry is quite clear, as we underlined in the brief section on marketing. Most of the issues covered are pretty universal and their implementation is only a matter of time.

Most studies relative to retail banking in particular, show that the deciding factor in banking is the way in which staff relates to both management and to the customer base. This course is about branch management in line with our belief that the whole difference between one bank and another one is predominantly its staff. Branch management is about their motivation, their know-how, and all the required qualities mentioned in this course so that, as a team in a branch, all can reach stated objectives.

Bibliography

P. Kotler and G. Armstrong: "Principles of Marketing", Prentice Hall International Editions ISBN 0.13.098039.0

R. Brealey & S Myers "Principles of Corporate Finance", Mc Graw Hill, ISBN 0.07.114053.0

Koontz & O'Donnell "Principles of Management", MC Graw Hill

J. Svigals: "Bank Branching 2010", Lafferty Publications, The Tower, IDA Centre, Pearse Street, Dublin 2, Ireland

J.L. Bauer: "Distribution 2000", Lafferty Publications,1996

Strategic Performance Management, Business Intelligence, 22-24 Worple Road, Wimbledon (SW19 4DD) UK – www. business intelligence.co.uk

P. Drucker, "Management: Tasks, Responsibilities, Practices", (New York; Harper & Row, 1973)

C. Ennew, T. Watkins & M. Wright: "Marketing Financial Services", Butterworth-Heinemann, Oxford, 1991

Financial Times, various articles

The Economist, various articles

D.F.Channon: "Bank Strategic Management and Marketing", John Wiley& Sons Ltd, 1992

Becker, Huselid and Ulrich, "The HR Scorecard", Harvard Business School Press, ISBN 1.57851.136.4

Robert Heller, "Achieving Excellence", Dorking Kindersley, ISBN 0.7513.0768.8

Robert Heller, "Essential Manager's manual", Dorking Kindersley, ISBN 0.7513.0400.X

Hyrum W. Smith, "Natural laws of successful time and life management", Time Warner AudioBooks, ISBN 0.446.51741.0

Robert T. Kiyosaki, S.Lechter "Rich Daddy, Poor Daddy", Time Warner, ISBN 0-7515-3271-1

David Cavell, "Branch Profitability", Lafferty, ISBN 1 86068 183 2

© by Promoculture ®   ISBN: 2-87974-069-X

Roger Jean Claessens

International lecturer in financial services

Ls. Sc. Comm. & Fin. (Applied economics) I.C.HEC, Brussels, Belgium.

Former Branch Manager with C.L.B.N. (Crédit Lyonnais Bank Nederland) in Rotterdam, Netherlands;

International professor at U.B.I., United Business Institutes, Brussels;

Official Senior Expert with A.T.T.F. the Financial Technology Transfer Agency, Luxembourg; lecturer for FEBELFIN (Belgian Finance Federation); the Banking and Finance Academy of Tashkent in Uzbekistan; International consultant with commercial and central banks for "Ethics, corporate values and the prevention of money laundering".

Philippe Wiertz

Licencié en criminologie de l'Université de Liège

4 years as Training Officer with Citibank (Certified - MBTI)

A years as Branch Manager with Citibank.

Currently Sales Manager Agent Network (22 agencies in South of Belgium)